GUIDANCE: 16-19

by the same author

The Teacher and Counselling
The Teacher and Pastoral Care
Problems and Practice of Pastoral Care (Ed.)
Teaching Study Skills

GUIDANCE: 16-19

Douglas Hamblin

BASIL BLACKWELL

Offered with humility to my students, who cared with discipline and creativity.

© Douglas Hamblin 1983
First published 1983

Reprinted 1986, 1987

Published by Basil Blackwell Ltd
108 Cowley Road
Oxford OX4 1JF
England

All rights reserved. No part of this publication may be reproduced, stored in a retrieval system, or transmitted in any form or by any means, electronic, mechanical, photocopying, recording or otherwise, without the prior permission of Basil Blackwell Limited.

All the material in this book remains subject to copyright but may be reproduced for classroom use only.

British Library Cataloguing in Publication Data

Hamblin, Douglas
   Guidance for the 16-19 age group.
   1. Personal service in secondary education
   I. Title
   373.14'0941   LB1620.5

   ISBN 0 631 13262 7
       0 631 13261 9 Pbk

Typeset in Plantin and Helvetica
by FD Graphics Limited
Printed in Great Britain

Contents

Introduction vii

1 : Issues and overview 1

2 : The techniques of guidance and counselling for the tutor 17

3 : Group guidance and counselling 44

4 : Adjustment to work, careers guidance and preparation for unemployment 67

5 : Group interaction and social skills 104

6 : Thinking about thinking and learning about learning 137

Epilogue 164

References 168

Index 173

Introduction

The education of the 16 - 19 age group is undergoing considerable development, much of it stemming from technological change and economic uncertainty. Traditionally, the relationship between teacher and taught takes a new and maturer form at this stage. This book tries to show the way in which this relationship can be extended by involving students as participants in their own guidance. Imposition and paternalism – even when the latter is benevolent – produce indifference, rejection and passivity in students. Allowing them to play a fuller part infuses a new vitality into guidance at this level. Much depends on the ethos of the institution and earlier learning experiences. Difficulties will arise, yet I believe that the effort will be fruitful. In another book I said that acts of faith were not necessarily acts of folly. That is worth repeating.

Current discussions of post-sixteen courses stress negotiation, contractual relationships and formative forms of assessment which put guidance and counselling at the heart of education. I hope that this book reflects these concerns to some degree.

Many students over the last thirteen years have contributed much to my own education. This book springs from our joint enterprises. My sincere thanks to them all. Frank Dickens was responsible for the original form of the cartoons in Chapter Five – I appreciate his kindness in allowing their reproduction. Thanks are inadequate for Edith Robinson, who typed the manuscript with care and interest. Her involvement was real and I offer her my gratitude.

Douglas Hamblin

1: Issues and overview

Summary points

> 1 The basic argument of this chapter is that guidance should be a negotiated rather than imposed activity.
> 2 Consumer research is essential. Students should not only be consulted but involved in the construction of activities.
> 3 Methods should be activity-based, involving small group work at times. Stress is laid on the need to consider developmental factors and the vulnerability of the 16-19 age group, who occupy a marginal position in society. Respect for the individual is the guiding principle behind any suggested activities.
> 4 Four basic modules, which form the centre of 16-19 guidance, are presented. These modules are:
>   Careers guidance and the issue of unemployment
>   Social and life skills
>   Group interaction
>   Learning about learning
> 5 The skills of counselling will have to be developed by tutors. Group counselling methods will have to be understood in some depth if guidance is to be productive.

A basic assumption

Imposition of guidance on the 16 - 19 age group will probably result in rejection and ridicule. Students may see it as demeaning, paternalistic or unwarranted interference. Application of unmodified programmes coming from outside the school or college invite routine and unthinking performance by tutors and superficial responses from students. Measures have to be taken to negotiate the content of the programme with students and stimulate their involvement. Meaningful guidance is a joint endeavour of student and tutor.

What factors have to be taken into account?

Pastoral care can be conducted with concern and integrity, and yet be made ineffective by unintended and unrecognised forces. Tutors are regarded as the agents through whom the care and and concern of the institution is made explicit. Yet, in practice, their work is often abortive, perhaps counter-productive. Why? Learning has occurred earlier in the secondary school which has often been negative in its cumulative impact. Unnoticed, the interaction between form tutor and the form has been weighted with activities that pupils see as negative: remonstrations about breaches of rules, especially uniform; administrative instructions; urging pupils to contribute to school projects; checks on truancy. Younger pupils interpret this as 'nagging', whilst older ones feel affronted because they lose dignity. Those responsible for 16 - 19 guidance inherit this legacy.

This view is not new. In *The Teacher and Counselling* (1974) it was pointed out that counselling services in schools create an image of those who use them in the eyes of staff, and more relevantly, peers. Adolescents can see counselling as allocating a deviant identity – they fear being labelled as nutcases. In one school a visit to the counsellor was referred to as 'going to the shrink'! This is poor practice rather than something inherent in the activity of counselling and guidance.

In a later chapter in the same work, Laing *et al* (1966) are cited. The implications of the 'pupil's view of the teacher's view of the pupil' were explored, showing how a pupil misinterprets the motives of the teacher who attempts to counsel. Discussion of the attributional and perceptual processes involved in counselling showed that pupils could reject it as an improper activity by the teacher, threatening to the pupil's dignity; or as irrelevant to the real issues of the pupil's life.

In that book it was also emphasised that counselling 'is not the prerogative of the dull, delinquent, disadvantaged, disturbed and deprived'. It is for all pupils, and provides the skills of coping with developmental tasks and the complexities of increasing maturity. These issues are germane to the development of guidance for the 16 - 19 age group in 1983. They are still unresolved because pastoral care has not abandoned the 'problem pupil' and 'inferior welfare system' approaches despite growing recognition that it is about learning (e.g., Welsh Office, 1982).

Students in the sixth form are alert to the danger that personal guidance can be, as Doherty (1977) reveals, a threat to personal autonomy and identity. Those who occupy a marginal role in the school, whose status in the family is uncertain, and who have a relationship with the larger society which contains many tensions, are sensitive to the expression and implications of authority in school or college. Curious evasions and contradictions have marked discussion and practice in guidance and pastoral care about the nature and exercise of authority. Emphasis is given to caring, yet in reality a counter-productive punitive element is strong in some schools, taking up most of the time of head of year or house (Doherty, 1977; Evans, 1982). More disturbing has been the denial of authority in pastoral care. Sixth form students are frequently aware that this has led to subtle forms of control, clothed in a language of caring and 'best interests' in which the pupil is manipulated into compliance. Authority, of course, does not mean the blind imposition of institutional goals or the absence of dialogue, but many of the 16 - 19 age group are sceptical about this, although they remain silent. Awareness of these reactions – and respect for them – must inform our attempts at guidance of this age group.

The curricular and the pastoral have been separated resolutely in some schools, yet this separation has been delusory. Curricular and pastoral activities occur within the same organisational structure and ethos. Poor pastoral care reflects a *malaise* in other aspects of teaching. For our purposes, it will suffice to register that the considerations noted above correspond to dilemmas which permeate school life. John (1980) draws attention to conflicts between:

1 teacher control and pupil independence;
2 competitive incentives and co-operative practice;
3 individuality and the sense of belonging to an institution.

Any experienced teacher will know that the unwelcome possibilities inherent in these alternatives assume a peculiar poignancy in relation to the 16 - 19 age group.

Mention has been made of the need to negotiate the guidance programme which also means we must have the notion of the hidden curriculum in mind. Hargreaves (1982) argues that the hidden curriculum in many schools destroys the dignity of pupils so pervasively that few recover from it. His viewpoints merit careful consideration by all involved in 16 - 19 guidance. Confusion of the new with what is good replicates the failure to distinguish between the desired and the desirable. If we let the baby out with the bath water there is a possibility that the result will be blocked drains! We may not have noticed what was lost during reforms. Hargreaves argues that we may have inflicted unnecessary deprivation on education through our repudiation of nineteenth century concern with the social functions of education. In an age of rapid technological and social change in which the signposts to the future are difficult to read, whilst long-term structural unemployment may have a profound impact on our lives, this warning should be taken seriously.

Perhaps we have assumed that if we strove to develop self-awareness, individuality and responsible autonomy, society would inevitably develop positively. Such a supposition is like that of the young people described by Berlin (1972), who believed that the sweeping away of existing social structures would inevitably lead to the emergence of a just society. Behind 16 - 19 guidance lies the need to equip young people to take up responsible roles in society although they may experience unemployment. A danger is that schools and colleges may be trapped into providing temporary palliatives or – worse still – pushed into a custodial role with the less able unemployed. *ABC in Action* (1981) registers the fact that some institutions find it difficult to meet the needs of the less able in pre-vocational training schemes, whilst appropriate courses in Further Education Colleges are becoming increasingly selective. Intellectual apartheid could occur as large numbers of the less able return to school, forcing schools to react by adopting non-developmental approaches to guidance.

Other tendencies could lead young people to reject guidance. Allocation of labels explains little and changes nothing. Explanations of behaviour and judgements of individuals incorporate an ever-present tendency in guidance to move from verbs to nouns, allocating an identity often difficult to refute. This shift from merely describing behaviour to making assumptions about personality is a major element in the disquiet about personal guidance shown by the sixth-form student.

Guidance therefore becomes self-defeating or ineffective unless we scan continuously and monitor the implications of what is offered. Counselling, which is to be at the heart of the new training initiatives, tended to divert blame from the institution to the individual. In their enthusiasm to understand, some counsellors or pastoral workers actually placed labels derived from psychiatric practice on pupils, showing a deterministic view of man which denied the developmental aims of education. A first step for those wishing to offer guidance to this age group is to begin to question their own assumptions.

Key questions for tutors

1 Does the guidance we intend to offer build a feeling of competence and extend a sense of *mastery in ways which are meaningful to the students?*

2 Is there a possibility that the guidance we offer now *strengthens passivity* and *increases reliance upon external checks and controls* instead of encouraging realistic responsibility?

> 3 What *hidden messages about the identity of this age group* are incorporated into the guidance, remembering that young people are vulnerable to self-doubt despite a well-developed talent for hiding it from others?

Why are the issues of trust and mistrust of great concern for the guidance of the 16 - 19 age group?

Rogers (1961) stated that 'trust is something which cannot be faked. It is not a technique.' The 16 - 19 age group experience deep concern with the issues of trust versus mistrust. They suspect the intentions of older adults, scanning the behaviour of their teachers critically, often focussing on the teacher's idiosyncracies or contradictory statements and actions. That this wariness extends to their peers is best illustrated by the sixth-form student who asked, 'Do you know how my friends define a secret? It is something you tell one person at a time!' Confidence had been breached by peers passing on information, whilst stressing on each occasion that it was to be regarded as a secret.

Many of those with whom I have worked have stressed their desire to trust, but their inability to do so with a sense of security. They seem to fear having identity or behaviours thrust upon them by those with whom they make a relationship. Conversely, they suspect, but find it hard to admit, a tendency in themselves to force others into roles or false positions. An image they frequently produce is that of themselves as a fortress which has to be defended against invaders. Defence of personal boundaries and protection of life space competes with the desire to share. Fears that others will misuse their honesty jostle with the desire to be open. Strategies designed to counter manipulation are the result.

In exploring the background to guidance it may be useful to focus on the difficulties at first, ignoring the vitality, aspiration and positive forms of egocentricity which are conspicuous features of the age group. Thus we become aware of the hidden curriculum behind the usual response, 'I'm here to get my qualifications and prepare for a career.' The major preoccupations of the individual's hidden curriculum centre on avoiding loss of face, coping with frustration, controlling self-doubt and dealing with anxiety as self-elected courses are pursued. The hidden curriculum produces rigidity and self-defeating attitudes, associated with misinterpretation of the motives of others and a resort to maladaptive behaviour. This hidden curriculum may be a product of their awareness that they hold marginal positions at home, at school and in relation to work and further or higher education. The ensuing susceptibility to social anxiety influences their acceptance of guidance. Let us recall that some of them may have learned negative things about pastoral care and tutor work – not least in importance that it involves you in trivial and embarrassing activities. They have then evolved ways of minimal response which successfully insulate them against tutor demands.

Birnbaum (1969), who was actively involved in promoting group work in schools, referred to the many tales of 'school systems and communities where bad situations have been made worse by the unintelligent application of inappropriate forms of sensitivity training.' Behind such warnings is yet another about the ease and conviction with which we can impose our conception of their needs on young people. Fostering maturity may mean that within *each institution* we must undertake consumer research. An on-going invitation to young men and women to define their needs and the relevant areas of guidance is a safeguard against imposition of the irrelevant.

Topics and methods can be suggested by writers but selection of what seems useful and the incorporation of additional material should be the joint endeavour of students and tutors. This is the meaning of the word 'negotiation' so frequently used in current discussion of 16 - 19 courses. In some schools guidance is seen as 'death by a thousand questionnaires'. The fact that each institution has its own value climate, organisation and history means that what works in one institution is ineffective in another. What is achieved in one school can be achieved in another, but through a different approach. Blind adoption of programmes leads to ritual performance by tutors who do not understand the purpose of activities. This in turn creates a group solidarity among students which strenuously resists innovation.

In summary, a dialogue between students and teachers is essential. Doubts and objections should be aired rather than stifled. Involvement of both sides in planning is essential, since post-compulsory education involves a contractual relationship, one that is essentially two-way. Imposition of programmes is unlikely to be successful with an age group which constantly scans its social environment for signals of derogation, and maintains a vigilant defence against pressures.

What are potential areas of guidance for the 16 - 19 age group?

1 *Careers guidance and preparation for long-term structural unemployment*
Careers education and unemployment at first sight appear to be unlikely bed-fellows. Proper caution must be exercised about

sweeping statements and predictions of the effect of microtechnology. Yet, as Taylor (1981) argues, it is clear that there will be a severe reduction in the demand for labour at all levels of skill, and in all areas of employment. Society has tended to see the handicapped as eternal children (Chapman, 1981), but there is an equally strong possibility that in the current climate of opinion the unemployed may be regarded as incomplete adults. The social and psychological implications of not having a job in our society, which is dominated by the work ethic, can be neither discounted nor ignored.

Careers guidance for this age group will focus on clarification of a life style in relation to both work and unemployment as a measure to reinforce the preservation of positive identity. We need to provide generic vocational skills which will enable students to cope with demands and pressures. Note that this programme is not so much concerned with the transition from school to work as with the difficulties and stresses which emerge in the first job.

Anticipation and innoculation are the basic principles employed in guidance both for adjustment in work and for coping with unemployment. Far from being negative or defeatist, the objective of such modules of guidance is to help students maintain themselves, cope adequately with stress, and use available resources, allowing them to enter employment, when it becomes available, with competence. Vocational skills will focus on the major impact of unemployment – the loss of the usual exchange relationship with society. Anthropological studies of small-scale societies, e.g. Mauss (1954), Malinowski (1922), have shown that such exchange relations are at the heart of social integration. Durkheim (1933) in his monumental study *The Division of Labour in Society* makes the same point impressively. Guidance programmes need to give the skills to make new forms of constructive exchange relationships as a means of preserving initiative, integrity of personality and self-respect during a period of unemployment. Entrepreneurial skills – a term used deliberately as emphasising risk-taking – need consideration in a guidance programme.

Further ideas will be given in Chapter 4. An outline of the areas which could form the basis for negotiation is given below:

Careers guidance and the issue of unemployment

1 The development of a satisfying life style. Ideas about the nature of success.
2 The skills of a job search and interview techniques.

3 The development of peer support groups, and the use of local agencies and facilities during a period of unemployment.
4 The skills of successful adjustment in first job.
5 Understanding family stresses and relationships in relation to unemployment. Sexual stereotypes and change induced by long-term structural unemployment.
6 Stimulation of initiative and the skills of creating your own job.

2 Social and life skills

Life skills is a popular, although ambiguous, term, possibly tinged with associations of inadequacy and inferiority in those who are the recipients of them. Yet in this 16 - 19 age group we have our future doctors, lawyers, teachers, clergy and others who will need the skills of communicating precisely and constructively with colleagues and clients. The skills of standpoint-taking, judgement and anticipating the reactions of others is a prime need for all this age group, whatever their ability and level of academic performance. Empathy or the ability to view a situation from the perspective of the other can be fostered. Like achievement motivation is not a black and white situation, i.e., *either* the individual has the capacity or skill *or* he has not, but a learned attitude accompanied by learned proficiencies rewarded in social interaction.

A good programme in which students are involved will contain real intellect and reinforce sound thinking. Lest this should sound elitist, I hasten to add that young people of all levels of ability think and reason adequately provided they are given relevant, concrete and realistic situations on which to concentrate. Some initial areas for exploration are:

Social and life skills

1 The examination of the factors which shape our judgements both of people and situations, distinguishing between inner forces and situational constraints.
2 Decision-making with particular attention to processing information, sources of influence and level of risk.
3 Social anxieties: sources of shame and embarrassment; loss of face; fear of revealing inadequacies; relationships with authority figures and self-defeating behaviours.
4 Tension management and reactions to anxiety.
5 Issues of self-fulfilment, the ideal for oneself and discrepancies between public and private selves.

A fascinating feature of this age group is the way in which earlier conflicts and developmental tasks acquire a new salience. In one sense, there is nothing new, although the content is more sophisticated. Increased susceptibility and reactions to old themes of trust and mistrust, initiative and passivity, shame, guilt and dependence emerged in counselling sessions I have taken. Over-simplification of the critical predicaments of young people about trust have to be avoided. Methods such as 'trust walks' should be cautiously evaluated. There is little evidence of any direct transfer of training to other social or personal situations. This, by itself, does not invalidate such approaches, as it may be the cumulative impact of a number of activities set in a context which is non-critical which induce change. This would certainly be the case with the approach to guidance presented in this book. Reservations are based on the fact that such methods fail to allow for some individuals having strong inhibitions about touching and being touched which are present very early in development, as Bell (1968), Fantz and Nevis (1961), Schaffer and Emerson (1964) and Snadowsky (1973) suggest in their researches. To ignore this possibility is to run the unnecessary risk of violating deep-seated feelings about personal space. What is pleasurable or acceptable to some is deeply threatening to others.

None of us would wish to produce young adults resembling the cool, calculated manager of impressions implicit in Goffman's (1959) analysis of social interaction. Even more distasteful would be the Machiavellian personality outlined by Christie and Geis (1970). Yet, as with other works by Goffman (1967; 1971), there is much that is illuminating. Our basic principle of respect means that we avoid exposure or threat, which might cause students to defend themselves by ridiculing the activities or opting out. We can, nonetheless, help them explore the consequences of:

1 undue or insufficient sensitivity to praise or criticism;
2 trust in authority or automatic rejection of it;
3 predictions and comparisons.

In a multi-cultural society undergoing rapid change it is imperative that young people understand the functions and dynamics of prejudice. Many are aware of their tendency to pre-categorise others, regret it, yet find themselves unable to change or inhibit it. The impact of extroversion and introversion could receive attention, exploring some of the myths about the desirability of one or the other.

Let me again remind the reader that such a module of guidance should be negotiated rather than imposed. Tutors should explain the importance of these areas, inviting students to assess what appears to be important. Negotiation would involve a joint working party who realise that this module must be seen in tentative terms and be subjected to close monitoring when in practice. Davies's (1976) concept of successive approximations with a continuous means/end dialogue is particularly appropriate here.

3 *Group interaction*

Group interaction remains a mystery to most young people. The most frequent complaint I meet is, 'Why do things go sour on me in a group? Why can't I put myself across as I really am?'. 16 - 19 year olds can also be over-dependent on their groups, simultaneously regretting that they feel powerless within it. The following themes preoccupy them.

> 1 Because I find membership of this group attractive, do I have to accept all its values?
> 2 Has the group the right to impose an identity upon me?
> 3 Why do I find myself forced to occupy a particular role?

Spivack *et al* (1976) produce evidence that the capacity to think about social casuality is related *positively* to tolerance of doubt and ambiguity, and *negatively* to anxiety and the tendency to indulge in evasive half-truths. They maintain that training in social problem-solving has been shown to decrease personal conflicts and to lower scores on tests of anxiety and insecurity. They claim that correlational evidence of quite a strong type shows that training in problem-solving aids adjustment. Two points emerge. Maladjusted adolescents seem to have a more restricted repertoire of solutions to everyday problems than others. This research also emphasises the fact that means/end thinking is intimately related to adjustment. This reinforces the insistence in this book that the ability to take the standpoint of others is a requisite for social and moral growth.

It may be helpful to introduce a brief discussion about what we mean by adjustment and normality. It is somewhat chastening to realise that we find it easier to talk about mental ill-health than positive mental health. Jahoda (1958) found it extremely difficult to define positive mental health clearly, but she does suggest some empirical indications we can use in 16 - 19 guidance. Mental health (or its opposite) is strongly associated with the attitudes the individual holds towards himself. It is also a partial function of the relationship of the person to his surroundings and life situation. A third component – one I believe to be crucial, and which good guidance should reinforce – is evidence of active attempts to master one's environment.

Klein (1960) took the discussion further, suggesting that mental health involves what she termed 'soundness'. This comprises the capacity to adapt to changes in circumstances, the ability to acquire and use social skills, the possession of initiative and a reasonable level of optimism. It also involves 'well being', which is the immediate or current level of ability to deal with stress.

These points, which poorly reflect the original discussions of Jahoda and Klein, provide an outline for the guidance process. If, as suggested by these writers, positive or negative attitudes towards oneself have important consequences for mental health, the self-exploration stressed in this overview is not self-indulgent but necessary for development.

The concept of normality is a key component of our judgements and implicitly underlies discussions of guidance. Those responsible for planning guidance for an age group which poses a challenge to the middle-aged should examine their definition of normality. They may find the normal person is similar to them, or that the concept of normality is derived from an idiosyncratic or narrow cultural base.

The statistical version of normality, i.e., the most frequently observed or most common type of behaviour, is used in one discussion, but in another the pejorative or moral aspects provide the the basic framework. Worse still is the situation where both are used interchangeably. The hidden question is about our conception of causality and determination. Does this lead us to under-rate students' capacity to change and take control of their destinies?

Self-respect is crucial for adjustment. Rosenberg (1979) argues very cogently from the perspective of those offering guidance to the 16 - 19 age group that the early years and first impressions are not necessarily the crucial ones. Why? He like many others, e.g. Rogers (1951), is using the self concept as the controller of change, and this develops relatively late. Older adolescents define themselves especially in terms of:

1 being attractive to others;
2 becoming attracted to others;
3 their strengths and weaknesses in interpersonal relationships.

These issues can be valuable areas of concern for the module on group interaction, for I have found that first-year sixth-form students often take up provocative and aggressive stances whilst ruminating almost obsessively about relationships and their acceptability.

We may not recognise, as Argyis and Schön (1974) argue, that gross discrepancies exist between what we do in group and interpersonal situations, and the 'espoused theory' which justifies and describes that behaviour. The role play, simulation and games used in guidance could break into this by systematically drawing attention to the following key variables:

Explanation	Predictions	Control
Propositions about why a certain pattern of behaviour exists and the function it serves for both the individual and group	Inferences about what will happen and the consequences	Propositions about change and how certain events can be made to occur

The consideration of causality which is advocated is not esoteric and should present no difficulty, for it is an inevitable part of life. Even those who lack academic orientation can analyse causality well when it is related to a real life situation. Heider (1967) argues that we all need to develop an orderly and coherent view of our social environment. This means that we need to go behind surface behaviours to the motives and intentions of the other person. We also need to consider the social contexts in which the behaviour occurs. Our focus is not on the behaviour as such, but on the motives and dispositions of other people. We, however, can be attributing these qualities falsely, therefore we are reacting to a figure who is partially our creation.

Guidance activities which raise questions about unstated assumptions, examine the way in which a specific situation seems to produce certain behaviours, and also explore young people's beliefs about what can be done to achieve desired results will serve them well. Therefore group guidance should emphasise cognitive problem-solving methods which allow students to verbalise their strategies for coping, and then submit them to further rational scrutiny.

Learned helplessness can be explored in relation to group interaction. Salient issues in the theory are:

1 the lack of a sense of control over what happens, i.e., powerlessness;
2 the belief that one's actions will not influence the course of events.

Those who feel this way either opt out or engage in superficial performance which enrages or irritates those who teach them. Garber and Seligman (1980) offer a fuller account of the phenomenon. It is important to state that a complex relationship which has not been fully explored exists between learned helplessness, internal versus external control, anxiety and achievement motivation. We can raise the issues, offering suggestions for coping, and allow young people to explore them in an accepting group guidance context. Our objective is the development of an orientation which welcomes challenge, and of a belief in their capacity to master events.

In negotiating the module on group interaction one might raise the following as areas of interest:

> **Group interaction**
> 1 Exploration of the nature of authority and leadership.
> 2 Understanding the power structure of groups.
> 3 Exploration of the mechanisms which operate in a group, scape-goating, bargaining, etc.
> 4 Analysis of the preferred roles taken up by individuals in the groups to which they belong.
> 5 Personal attraction.
> 6 Conflicts and decision-making in groups.
> 7 Approval and affiliation needs.
> 8 Co-operation, competition and productivity in groups.

4 *Learning about learning and problem-solving*
In some ways this section recapitulates what has gone before, for guidance is basically conceived as a learning process. In this module, the learning is related to academic work.

Attention should be paid to rigidities which influence learning, both self-imposed and springing from external restraints. One would hope that the mechanics of study had been established, but crash courses on note-taking and other basic skills of study will probably be needed. Ideally, preferences for learning, individual patterns of coping with stress and disliked tasks and exploration of work patterns should form the object of discussion.

In relatively non-directive forms of group counselling which embody activities the following could be the focus in the early stages:
 1 defences against learning;
 2 ideas of the nature of success;
 3 the influence of perceptions and self-evaluation on achievement.
The impact of new demands, plus the uncertainty of the future, seduce some students into doubting and rejecting their individual aspirations. Our objective in this module of guidance is to integrate thinking and feeling, producing a tough-minded, constructive

resolve to rise above circumstances. This will include rigidity which creates frustration. Rubenowitz (1963) demonstrated that this was a pervasive frame of mind, relatively independent of intelligence, which influenced evaluation of ideas and activities, and shaped judgements of music and art.

It should be made clear that the foregoing is not justification for an attempt to impose any specific system of critical thinking or creativity on students. This again would be a violation of dignity. People have different styles of thought. The objectives are limited: to encourage students to raise relevant questions about their style of thought and problem-solving; to identify feelings associated with poor performance; to look at evasive mechanisms and self-defeating ways of working. The responsibility is theirs alone, and the style of learning is unique to each individual in some respects. The old adage that one man's meat is another man's poison holds good in the field of learning. One would hope that an open approach which questions what they are offered and how they react would develop.

Questions examining beliefs about causality can be raised. Self-diagnosis, evaluation and strategies for achievement will form part of the debate. Individuals can be unwittingly in collusion with the forces that prevent them achieving their goals. Care will be needed to avoid reinforcing helplessness and passivity, but the effect is worthwhile.

In evaluation of learning style, the implications of concrete thinking should be brought out. Hoggart (1959) suggests that some individuals –

1. tend to make extreme and polarised judgements, resisting evidence that might modify their position;
2. rely on status and power as a basis for their judgements;
3. are relatively insensitive to cues emanating from others;
4. tend to generalise about others from incomplete judgements.

This list clearly shows the ways in which the intellectual and social intermingle. All the items can be related to decision-making in a job or group.

The need to select the salient, and to reduce the redundant or irrelevant elements in a learning task has to be brought to the forefront of activities and discussions on learning. Inferential thinking and the use made of evidence will have to be examined. But we need to beware guidance procedures which accentuate existing divisiveness. The partial answer lies in reliance on small group work which embeds problem-solving in *concrete situations*, and allows students taking different courses to share ideas and widen one another's perspectives. This is accompanied by the insistence that in many areas of life there are no 'right answers', merely conditional and propositional statements which never contain the ultimate truth. The tutor's concern that students should develop their own method of processing information, and his demonstration of respect for it reduce the risk of potential conflict. The module concerned with learning and problem-solving could include:

> **Learning about learning**
>
> 1 Work on problem-solving. Understanding reactions and techniques.
> 2 Questioning assumptions.
> 3 Rigidity and early closure.
> 4 Using evidence and drawing conclusions.
> 5 Self-diagnosis.
> 6 Planning skills.
> 7 Processing what has been learned.
> 8 The skills of an information search.
> 9 Developing logical arguments.
> 10 The constructive use of imagination.

A note on methods

Modules have been suggested as the basic unit of organisation. This has certain advantages:
1 revision of content is easier;
2 tutors have greater flexibility because they can change the sequence with less inconvenience;
3 as the number of units is increased, the opportunity exists to involve more students in the planning.

Negotiation involves tentativeness which is not necessarily an aimless condition. Those responsible for guidance can gradually adjust methods and content to fit the needs of students, bearing in mind the fact that students question what we do if it is not obviously related to the task of the institution as they perceive it. Legitimacy of guidance, like trust, has to be earned. Part of our task is to educate students, parents and the wider public about the nature and importance of guidance.

Each activity must have objectives, which should be communicated to the students. Active methods involve small group activities of various types. Tutors may be alarmed by this, unfamiliarity with the approach causing them to anticipate difficulties in an exaggerated way. Provided that the activities are clearly structured, and students allowed to select their partners or small group, the method is less noxious for the student than the one where the tutor tries to blandish or coerce individuals to express their opinions in front of the total group. Active approaches demand good classroom management, which is a basic professional skill for the teacher, not an alien imposition. Readers will find the thoughtful discussion by Watkins (1981) of assistance.

The tutor will need to develop the skills of individual and group counselling. Some help will be given with this in Chapters 2 and 3. Within each institution in-service training will be necessary for productive guidance if the current laudable statements are to become a reality. Undoubtedly, teachers and lecturers have real concern for the needs of students. What is not so certain is whether we currently possess the knowledge and skill to translate the value into practice.

2: The techniques of guidance and counselling for the tutor

Summary points

> 1 Three basic skills are introduced which are the basis of effective communication in a helping situation.
> 2 Diagnostic and behavioural counselling techniques which rest on good teaching skills are introduced.
> 3 The importance of standpoint-taking is stressed throughout the chapter.
> 4 The techniques are related to case histories, selection of responses and a strategy for investigating underfunctioning.
> 5 The limitations of the work of the tutor in relation to the family are made clear.

Introductory note

In this exposition, which is a limited one, guidance will be seen as a generic term. Counselling is a helping activity carried out by the tutor as part of guidance.

Three basic skills

The Further Education Curriculum Review and Development Unit has consistently stressed, e.g., (1981; 1982), the central relationship of counselling to the pre-vocational course. The alert tutor is painfully aware that attempts at helping may produce no more than socially desirable verbal responses unbacked by intent to act. Superficiality or evasiveness by the student is often the outcome of much alleged counselling.

Realistic assessment of difficulties must inform guidance. Ahlstrom and Havighurst (1971) produce rather gloomy evidence in their study of four hundred adolescents. In their experiment, which offered half the day at work, and the replacement of normal school routines by a specially designed programme, they found little positive response. Some of the participants manifested a restless search for excitement, and it was obvious that a special programme could not compensate for the experience of growing up in a society which did not provide responsible roles for the disadvantaged and offered little experience of meaningful success in school. Some individuals responded well to the work experience, but Ahlstrom and Havighurst report that workers were not able to touch a sub-group who displayed an aimless drifting without regard for their futures or even their current life situations. In counselling, the tutor must remember that some students have built up status by developing reputations as tough, virile and worldly-wise males or females. But this is superficial in many cases. Fear of loss of face, of ridicule or being singled out as inferior or different underlies the façade. They bring with them the theme of unfair treatment and the desire to get even. They will sometimes respond to responsible and competent adults who make them feel accepted and give recognition.

Inarticulate students are particularly sensitive to the context or setting in which communication occurs. For them the formal interview is also likely to be contaminated with associations of trouble. Attitudes of belligerence and defence are automatically aroused. Negative expectations not only prevent them from using the tutor, but distort their perception of his responses, which they interpret as repudiation of them. If family background has taught them to regard authority figures as the 'them', who neither understand their difficulties nor possess sympathy for them, they close their minds to the help of the tutor. The three basic skills outlined prevent the tutor from confirming these beliefs, and help build communication.

The first basic skill
LOOK FOR THE STUDENT'S FEELINGS BUT AVOID RELIANCE ON CLOSED QUESTIONS

Questions which suggest the answer we expect or which can be answered by 'Yes' or 'No' prevent us from learning what a problem is about. Closed questions result in the tutor:
   1 having to ask yet another question, turning what should be helpful into a process of probing or interrogation;
   2 creating a situation in which the student tells you what (s)he thinks you want to hear rather than the facts;

3 producing from the student a series of polite non-committal responses of the 'Don't know' type. The well-intentioned tutor then tells them what they ought to know. Students can then ignore this as irrelevant with a good conscience.

As we look for the feelings we learn to *reflect back*, i.e., to repeat that part of the student's response which contains important statements. Two dramatic, true examples illustrate the technique:

Example 1

Student A 16 year-old female from a good social background.

Jane 'May I talk to you about my father? He's started going out every night, drinks heavily and comes in late. Then he starts hitting mother, and I'm so worried.'

Tutor 'So worried, Jane?'

Jane 'Yes, I don't think he knows when to stop. I'm afraid he'll go too far one day and . . .'

Example 2

Student A 17 year-old male who has good ability and no apparent problems.

John 'Do you think I can afford to take a year off before I go to college? Living in my village is like living in a glass box with everybody watching you.
What do you advise me to do?'

Tutor 'Living in a glass box with everybody watching you, John?'

John 'Oh well! I'll tell you about it. Last year my elder brother mucked about with a girl up on the hillside, and eventually got sent down. There's only Mum and Dad and me at home. They think the village is still talking about it – and, do you know, sir, I feel they are waiting to see what I'm going to do.'

The examples show that focusing on feelings allowed the key issues to emerge. It is not always as simple or immediate as this but the technique is the key to good guidance.

> *The second basic skill*
> SEND A SIGNAL OF ACCEPTANCE IMMEDIATELY

This prevents the arousal of unnecessary defensiveness in the student. Brusque or unaccepting initial statements make the student cling to his standpoint resolutely, or even induce him to move to a more extreme position.

> ## Example 3
>
> *Situation*   A student has done badly in an examination where she was expected to do well. She is therefore vulnerable.
>
> *Tutor's initial response*
>   'You must feel very puzzled, Jean. You worked so hard and we all expected you to do well. It must be hard to take.'
>
> The statement of acceptance should reflect the reality of the student's feelings as accurately as possible.
>
> ## Example 4
>
> *Situation*   An A-level candidate is insisting on choosing a subject for which the prognosis of success is unfavourable. He appears determined to take it at all costs.
>
> *Tutor's initial remark*
>   'I can see that taking this subject means a great deal to you, Bob. I really appreciate how you feel, but perhaps we can look at it together.'
>
> Without this message it is probably that the student would resort to blind defence of his decision. Even with the signal of acceptance there will still be difficulties, but a basis for counselling has been established.

> *The third basic skill*
> AVOIDING CONTRADICTIONS IN MESSAGES AND SCORPION COMMUNICATION

Bateson *et al* (1956) produced the idea of double-bind in communication. For our purposes it can be described as communication where two contradictory messages are sent to the student about something so important that he cannot ignore them.

Example 5

Situation The tutor is talking to an anxious student taking O-levels in the near future.

Statement 'Well, Carole, I know you will do well in your O-levels, but don't worry if you fail. There is another chance in November.'

Out of context, this sounds banal. Yet I have heard this statement frequently. The vulnerable student registers the unintended sting in the tail. She leaves feeling that a superficial attempt to cheer her up has been made, but that the tutor really expects her to fail. We then label the pupil as anxious, wondering why our reassurance does not help.

Example 6

Situation The student has a problem about academic work.

Student 'Well, I would work harder, if only my mother didn't nag so!'

Tutor 'Yes, but . . .'

This is the most damaging form of contradiction. At one level we signal that we are accepting and trying to understand the viewpoint of the student. Then, before we have discovered what the problem is, we say, 'Yes, but . . .' The student feels we are imposing our definition of the problem or arguing with her. She then opts out, telling her friends there is no point in talking to us.

Interview techniques

Counselling is claimed to be central in the new development for the 16 - 19 age group in conjunction with profiles which form the basis of formative assessments through which targets are revised and progress is monitored. This means the tutor has to sharpen his interview skills. Tutorials are less effective than they should be, usually because the tutor talks too much, whilst the student is passive. But abstention from unnecessary talk is insufficient for guidance. The structure of the interview needs to be examined.

A   *Preliminary stage*

Preliminary crystallisation of objectives is essential. Objectives are not final statements, but merely give a direction. 'What do we hope will be the outcome of the interview?'

B   *Input*

We ask:
1 What information do we have about the student? What is our reaction to it? How valid is the information? Examination of credibility of the source and its status cannot be neglected. Is it hearsay or does it have a more reliable status?
2 What information do we need to obtain from the student? How can this be done economically?
3 We must ask what perceptions the student is likely to hold of the interview. Is he likely to see it as constructive or destructive, legitimate or illegitimate? What stereotypes exist on both sides?

C   *Interaction*

Quickly assess:
1 Is the status of the tutor to be stressed?
2 Who will be active in what ways?
3 Are the issues of trust or confidentiality likely to enter?
4 Will certain activities take precedence, e.g., fact-finding, exploration of feelings or perceptions, or clarification of the nature of a problem.

D   *Output*

Good counselling is based on a clear idea of what the output will be. Some modifications will occur during the interview, but the sense of purpose is vital. Ask if it is hoped to:
1 develop the student's ability to cope with a situation by giving him the skills;
2 help him to see the situation differently;
3 come to a decision as to the actions he should take?

These points can be encapsulated into a simple interview structure. The three stages provide a framework for the tutor to assess his efficiency. (See the diagram opposite.)

It is common to find a confusion between rapport and a relationship. The former is the climate of warmth and acceptance which is a pre-requisite for communication. The latter is based on trust which has to be earned, and is a product of the student's growing confidence in the tutor as they work together.

Be clear that guidance does not remove the responsibility from the

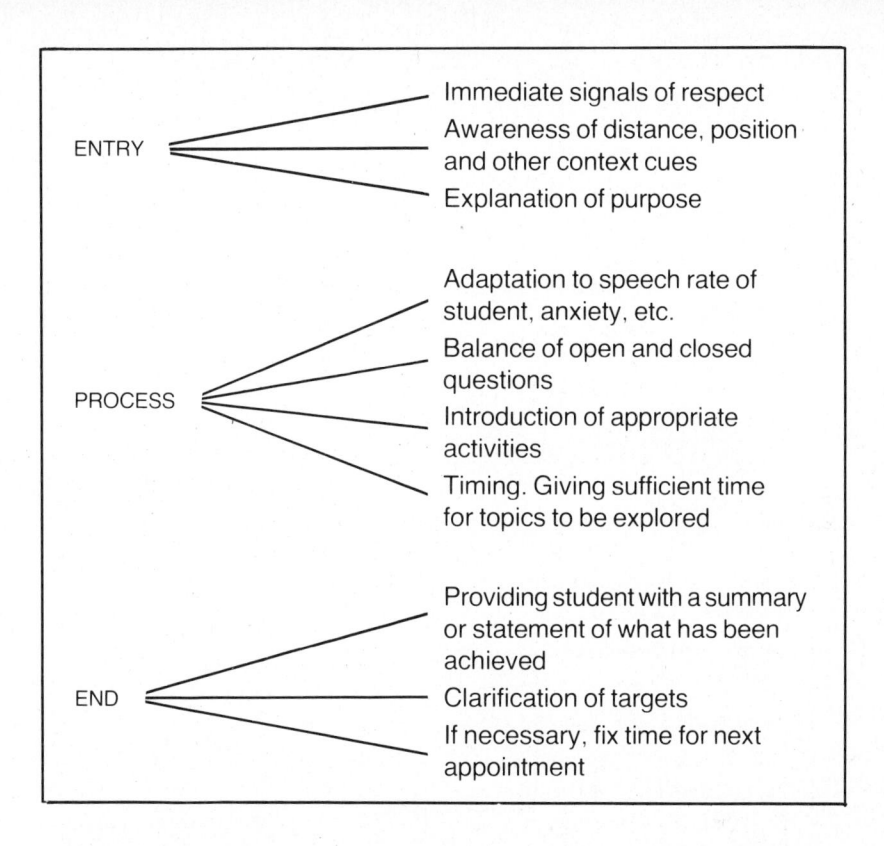

```
ENTRY ─────┬──── Immediate signals of respect
           ├──── Awareness of distance, position
           │     and other context cues
           └──── Explanation of purpose

PROCESS ───┬──── Adaptation to speech rate of
           │     student, anxiety, etc.
           ├──── Balance of open and closed
           │     questions
           ├──── Introduction of appropriate
           │     activities
           └──── Timing. Giving sufficient time
                 for topics to be explored

END ───────┬──── Providing student with a summary
           │     or statement of what has been
           │     achieved
           ├──── Clarification of targets
           └──── If necessary, fix time for next
                 appointment
```

student. The skill of the tutor rests in his ability to help the student see how he contributes to the maintenance of the state of affairs of which he complains.

The following are common sources of inefficiency in interviews:

1 Asking double-barrelled questions

We may have developed the habit of asking two or more questions consecutively. If acquiescence is signalled, we are satisfied. Yet we cannot be sure whether the agreement is with both questions or only one. We can then follow up with yet another question creating further unrecognised distortion.

2 Interruption

Again it is easy to interrupt, cutting off the student's flow of thought and re-directing it.

3 Assumptive statements

This means that we anticipate what the student is going to say, or even worse, tell him what we think he is wanting to say. This hides a more serious assumption of similarity between ourselves and the student. A false assumption of similarity of feelings or reaction destroys our ability to help.

4 Failure to adapt

If we wait for the anxious student to speak because we feel our task is to listen, then we increase anxiety. With some students we need to talk a lot, structure the situation by asking questions, providing nods or grunts of encouragement. Some students will need eye contact and some will hate it. Our task is to observe and adapt.

An exercise

The reader may find it useful to attempt the exercise on selection of responses. There is no single right answer. It is intended to help you scan more widely. The first statement will be familiar. (This is developed from the valuable discussion of Allen and Whiteley, 1968.)

Counselling training – selection and evaluation of responses

Instructions
Below you will find a statement made by a student, which is followed by a number of responses a tutor could make. You are asked to consider these carefully and then select the one you think is the best. Put a ring round the number of that response.

Indicate in the space given your reasons for choosing that response.

1 *Student statement*
'Well, I did think about being a doctor, but, as I keep saying, I do want to travel. It seems I've got to get these things together somehow, so I might do research after qualifying. That would let me get around. I feel as if I've lived in a little glass box cooped up in my valley and my family gets on my nerves. I can learn a lot by travelling and I ought to see things. I suppose everybody of my age says this, but . . .'

Tutor responses
a So you're really more interested in medicine than any other career?
b It is very important that we see if you are tackling your preparation for a medical career in the best possible way.
c Your school work is going to be pretty important if you really want to do this.
d It looks as if you might feel confused and boxed in, and you may wish you knew more about what you are doing.
e Yes, it is important to get your plans sorted out, at your age you can't afford to drift around.
f Perhaps you really feel you must break out of these patterns of living in which you get caught up and which don't seem meaningful to you.
Reason for choice

1 *Student statement*
You know I've got this idea in my head that I have to stick it out. I've made a decision and it hasn't turned out to be the right one, so it's best to stick to it. Or perhaps it isn't, you know. It may be harder to learn that you can make a mistake in deciding, but you don't have to stick to it.
Tutor responses
a Yes, I tend to agree with you.
b Sometimes we feel it's a good thing to stick to a decision even though another looks better, just as if there were some special virtue in sticking to things.
c Could it be that there's something at the back of your mind that says you ought to stick to it?
d We should sort this out. You won't be able to see things straight if this muddle continues.
e Lots of people feel like this at your age, but don't worry – these things sort themselves out as you grow up.
f Perhaps these situations are not as important as we think they are.
Reason for choice

3 *Student statement*
I suppose I could take my O-levels again, but it may be better to take fewer – eight seemed too many for me. I don't know, I'm a

bit afraid of facing this load or failing. Perhaps if I try I'll feel able to do the whole lot.

Tutor responses
a   You mentioned the Youth Club just now. Do you think going there was the cause?
b   You'll begin to feel better once you see some sign of improvement somewhere.
c   What's this about? All the evidence I have suggests you can do well if you really try.
d   Do you think you might be saying that once the load reaches a certain point you feel swamped and can't cope any longer?
e   Shall we begin to think about ways of improving your working and study habits and putting this right?

Reason for choice

4   *Student statement*
Perhaps most girls are like it, but I seem to get depressed a lot. Mother does take me to the doctor and I get tablets, but I can't go on taking them because I might get . . . what do you call it? . . . I shouldn't be able to do without them, and I don't want to be like that.

Tutor's responses
a   Well, you could try taking tablets sometimes and not at others, and then you won't get dependent upon them.
b   What is it that makes you depressed in the first place?
c   Perhaps you resent the fact that you get false happiness and good feelings from the tablets and wish you were really happy?
d   It probably means that you'd like to be able to do something about this yourself. Is it that you wish you didn't have to accept both the unpleasant feelings and the tablets . . . that you could do something yourself?
e   Perhaps if you concentrate on putting right things that go wrong you wouldn't get depressed. Shall we begin by looking at the Youth Club?
f   Obviously you are quite right not to want to become dependent upon the tablets. You need to begin to tackle the problem in a realistic way.

Reason for choice

5 *Student statement*
All my life I've felt inferior to my older brother because I've had to compete with him. He has always been first in his class, plays for the school in rugby and I'm useless and no good by comparison with him.

Tutor's responses
a I see, the problem is that you feel inferior.
b I wonder if we could look at this more closely, perhaps there are important things we could explore together?
c Well, it is a fact of life that older brothers tend to do better at things just because they are older.
d Part of life and living means accepting the fact that we can't always do as well as other people.
e This seems very clear to me and my job is to help you come to terms with this situation.
f Self-pity isn't very helpful in this situation, you've got to get yourself out of it very quickly.
g Your feelings must be very painful, perhaps especially because he is your brother.

Reason for choice

6 *Student statement*
It's the old man . . . he keeps on and on. I bet he was worse than me at my age, but he's forgotten what it's like to be young. That's the trouble with all adults, they're all the same.

Tutor's responses
a Yes, I know how you feel, but most young people feel as you do.
b Your father has done a lot for you and you should really try to see things from his point of view.
c Fathers are like that. They just don't try to understand how their sons feel.
d Perhaps you are feeling lost and upset and that nobody takes the trouble to understand you.
e It sounds as though you might feel that everybody is against you. I wonder in what way I come into this?
f Cheer up, it isn't as bad as all that.
g What's it like to be young?

Reason for choice

Now go back and *In less than a minute* put a cross against the response you are sure you wouldn't use. Don't stop to think about it. Discussion of the reasons for *not* selecting a response are at least as valuable as the reverse.

Behavioural counselling

Counselling is a process in which one person helps another change his feelings, attitudes and behaviour so that they yield more satisfying outcomes to him and to others. Note that this emphasis on the social nature of counselling relates to the comments of Hargreaves (1982). It also stresses that behaviour should become more satisfying. Teachers can behave in counselling as if the sole object were to get information or be the recipient of confidences. Observation suggests a confusion of means and ends. One has the impression that the objective is solely getting the student to tell the tutor about the problem, whereas the crucial step is what is done once the problem is known. A behavioural approach is necessary because it:

1. tailors strategies and actions to the needs and situation of the student;
2. requires the tutor to help the student think about a problem in ways which allow him to detect the steps that have to be taken to resolve it;
3. takes a concrete approach, avoiding reliance on vague abstractions such as 'aggressive' or 'inadequate'. We are pushed to look at the situations in which the aggression or inadequacy appear, and the form they take. A plan for dealing with difficulties, based on 'one step at a time', is constructed. This rids guidance of amorphousness and destroys the validity of the student complaint, 'They tell me I must change, but not how I am to do it.' Responsibility is still present because the student is involved actively in planning the steps. Krumboltz and Thoresen (1969) and Thoresen and Mahoney (1974) are among many writers who suggest that this involvement should be linked to a mutual contract. This is in line with the current emphasis in planning pre-vocational courses.

The key concept is *reinforcement*. It is salutary to ask oneself habitually, 'What have I strengthened in this person?' at the end of an interview. Reinforcements are the equivalent of rewards which strengthen a tendency or behaviour. Often they are unintended – in the classroom we can self-defeatingly pay more attention to the behaviours of which we disapprove than those which we hope to encourage. We should beware of paying attention to the negative at the cost of the positive.

Extinction is concerned with the elimination of undesired behaviours. Behaviours often disappear when they are not rewarded. In both individual and group counselling situations, the tutor should be aware of the behaviours he intends to reward and those which he will ignore. If a student says, 'Well, you won't change my mind', to challenge it is to strengthen it.

The idea of a *hierarchy* is useful. In cases of situational anxiety or where the student has to acquire a number of skills, tutor and student can arrange them in order of intensity of reaction in the former, and of difficulty in the latter. The sensible approach is 'one thing at a time', dealing first with the least anxiety-provoking or easiest item. This builds a sense of mastery.

Stimulus generalisation means that feelings and reactions associated with a specific person, object or situation have spread to another. These situations are similar to the original one in some relevant way, e.g., an adolescent who has a hostile relationship with his step-father may begin to extend that hostility to middle-aged teachers without any provocation from them. Failure in one subject can extend to another. The good subject becomes associated with the stressful one, and performance in it deteriorates. It is best described as contamination by association.

A behavioural approach takes the above into account, and asks the tutor to assess with the student:

Basic behavioural assessment
1 Which behaviours need to be increased in frequency or intensity?
2 Which behaviours should be reduced in intensity or frequency?
3 What new behaviours should be acquired?
4 What behaviours must be eliminated?
5 What factors in the student's life space present difficulties?
6 What supports are present in the environment which can be used?

Tutors need to think in terms of tactics and strategies, rather than recipes. They must ask themselves, 'What will work with this student?' The student, of course, is involved. Then the tutor should:
1 check that the targets are meaningful to the student;
2 break the long-term target down into intermediate steps;
3 present the mutually agreed plan for achieving the goal so that the student grasps what has to be done;

4 teach any necessary skills as they are required or ensure that someone else teaches them.

Diagrams and simple charts can be used to make the steps clear. Behavioural counselling has two advantages for the tutor. As it centres on concrete behaviours arranged in a step-by-step pattern, the student can see his success. It makes no unusual demands on the tutor because it employs the skills of teaching.

What is not so obvious is the shift from consequences to the antecedents of behaviour, a move which leads to prevention rather than cure. Consequences of behaviour have to be examined, but for self-control we need to alert students to the point at which difficulties arise. When do they feel the desire to opt out of a lesson? When do they feel they cannot be bothered to tackle an assignment? Which situations in the classroom bring loss of face and how does the student react? If the tutor helps students identify 'trigger' situations, and then behave constructively at that point, conflict does not escalate, and habitual negative patterns of behaviour can, first, be interrupted and, second, be replaced by more effective behaviours. This is shown in the following case history:

Mandy – a victim of 'trigger' situations

The situation Mandy, who is at a good further education college, had a violent row with a teacher. She was suspended for three weeks but has requested to return. The college is a good one, priding itself on the quality of its caring. The Vice-Principal has asked the counsellor to work with her.

Counselling The counsellor was concrete and specific. Mandy explored what happened on the day of the row. She drew up a diagram after 15 minutes' discussion which showed these points:

1	*Where it began*	When I came in late. But I didn't mean to be late!
2	*What made it worse*	It was Miss Jones who told me off. I like her, and she doesn't usually tell me off.
3	*The last straw*	That girl laughing at me. I went mad, banged my desk lid and called Miss Jones a nasty name.

This seems logical, but the counsellor was awake to the possibility that these situations contained latent significance. Therefore he

asked Mandy to tell him more about:
1. *The first trigger.* How had she behaved in the past when she had meant to do something, and then had done something but not meant to do it? It seemed that Mandy had strong, somewhat primitive concepts of intent and justice, which were:
   a If she had meant to do it, she accepted rebuke;
   b If she had not meant to do it, she felt the lecturer should accept her statement. If it was not accepted, she started to argue violently.

   Mandy had to be taught to behave differently in this trigger situation. She blindly assumed that the lecturer would accept her lateness because she had not intended to be late. The girl had to be taught to take the standpoint of the teacher.

2. *The second trigger.* Here Mandy gave examples of the way she reacted when disciplined by teachers she liked or disliked. The upshot seemed to be that criticisms were accepted when they came from people she did not like. If she liked them, she felt her liking was a reward for them, and they should not tell her off. Again, there was evidence that this trigger led to trouble.

   Mandy had to be taught to look maturely at the situation and learn to control her initial impulse to argue.

3. *The third trigger.* This was vital. Mandy was tall, heavy, almost muscular and raw-boned. She could not accept this. Her illustrations showed she was vulnerable to laughter from girls. (It seemed she had the boys in her group under control.) But if a girl laughed at her she would do anything to re-establish her dominance.

   Mandy had to be taught not to respond in ways which gave the other girl a pay-off. She was taught to use humour sensibly, and also to present herself more attractively physically. The counsellor had the impression she had given up trying to be attractive.

This case was unusual because the cumulative impact of three consecutive trigger situations led to a major problem.

Standpoint-taking and clarifying a problem

Tutors must not impose their assessments of the nature of problems on students. Tentative suggestions can be made, but tutors have to suspend temporarily their viewpoint, and adopt that of the student. Behaviour is partially a result of how we see things. Often we do not realise how great the differences in perception can be. Each one of us holds expectations about the behaviour of others, whilst our behaviour is a product partially of our predictions. Each problem is unique because of the interpretation placed on it by the individual. To ignore the standpoint of the student is to risk giving absurd, if not harmful, advice.

Standpoint-taking is the building up of a coherent view of the student's position from his incoherencies, low level signals, occasional contradictions as well as his straightforward statements. Tutors have to train themselves to think in terms of hypotheses, retaining the power to modify as more evidence becomes available. Suspension of judgement is prime, because the problem as it appears initially may be incomplete, obscuring more fundamental difficulties. Advocating a behavioural approach does not mean ignoring perceptions or emotions or seeing them as merely concomitants of behaviour.

Tutors who offer developmental guidance should appreciate the pressures on the student and the network of expectations and obligations which shape behaviour. The three basic skills allow one to discover the structure and meaning of a problem. But people do not live in a vacuum – therefore the context has to be examined. Learning or personal problems are affected by people in the student's life space. Parents' or friends' reactions can be more problematical for the student than the actual problem.

Let us now look at putting a sense of being in control back into the student. First, we could ask him to observe systematically his behaviours and feelings for three days. Attention should be paid to:

1 his beliefs about others' motives and the likely course of events;
2 how the situation or feelings begin;
3 the way in which he coped;
4 the reaction of other people to his coping.

With care, this will create a realistic climate for attack on the problem, selecting the salient elements. The idea of a hierarchy leads to the principle of graduation. Arranging things in increasing order of difficulty gives structure and makes the student feel in control. Tackling the easiest element first promotes confidence. Students are helped to discuss their plan for coping, articulate it clearly, and finally, in conjunction with the tutor, anticipate snags. These self-instructions are learned as the first step in coping. Decision-making theory draws the following to our attention in a useful way:

Components of the decision-making process

Awareness	Need to make a decision
	Individual elements
	Relationship between these elements

Choice   Recognition of alternatives

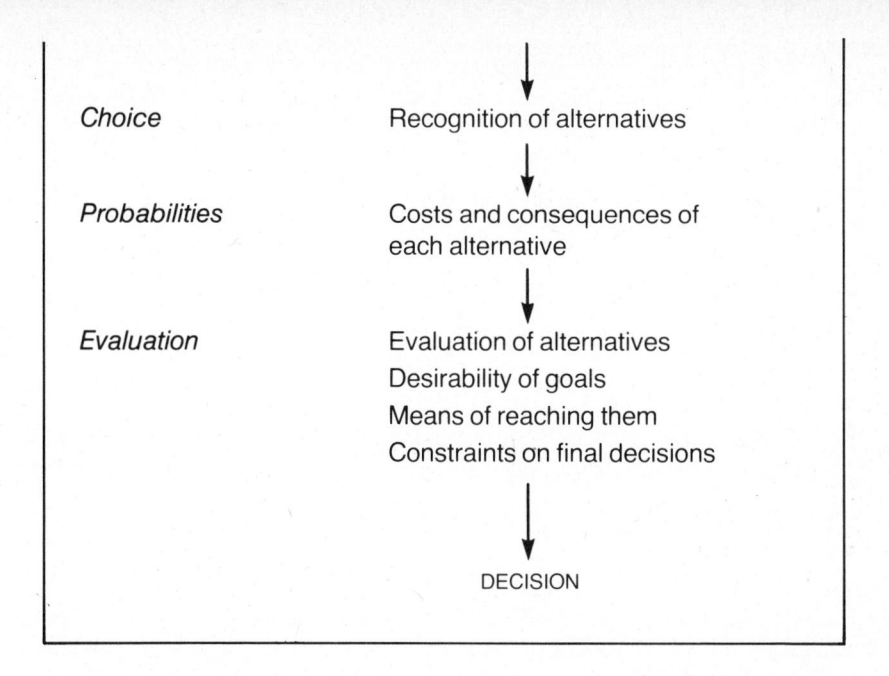

Probabilities   Costs and consequences of each alternative

Evaluation   Evaluation of alternatives
                               Desirability of goals
                               Means of reaching them
                               Constraints on final decisions

                                         DECISION

A checklist of skills associated with good counselling for the tutor

Tutors will find it helpful to ask themselves how effective they are in using the areas of the checklist. Other profitable questions are:
1 What are the implications of weakness in a particular area?
2 How can I boost my skill?

This checklist will also provide a basis for training groups of tutors.

DO I:
1 Signal respect and concern to the student?
2 Build on the strengths of the student?
3 Make constructive use of open questions?
4 Allow the student to participate in planning the course of action?
5 Show warmth?
6 Draw constructive attention to the student's feelings?
7 Encourage the student to elaborate what he is saying?
8 Consider impact of my facial expression and voice quality on student?
9 Deliberately reinforce attempts at change?
10 Pace the interview carefully, adapting to the needs of the student?

An illustration. Underfunctioning – a strategy for the tutor
This section will be used to explore an important problem, but it also illustrates the application of the earlier part of this chapter. In the current climate, post-compulsory education is meeting many problems associated with learning, motivation and underfunctioning. Attention is drawn to the elements of thought needed for effective guidance.

1 *The need to question assumptions*
Despite frequent use as an evaluation of performance, underfunctioning is a remarkably vague concept. This may stem from its complexity, for attitudes, learning preferences, lack of specific intellectual skill and perception of the relevance of school are involved. Judgements of underfunctioning often turn out to be highly subjective. Naive beliefs about the innate nature of ability and the anticipated attainment of students from good social backgrounds shape assessments. Rarely are they submitted to rational scrutiny.

2 *Basic issues*
Underfunctioning seems to imply the existing of some objective standard, i.e., some level to which a pupil should be raised. But is this realistic? The idea that a ceiling to performance not only exists but can be recognised is doubtful. Links between intelligence and attainment are weaker than we often think. Whilst there is a tendency for high intelligence and high performance to be associated, we must recall that a trend is not a direct relationship. Many variations and minor contradictions exist within the broad tendency. Learning is subject, amongst other things, to the motivational state of the student, the characteristics of both teacher and subject, and the learning context. The latter includes the influence of peers who may set a limit to achievement, operating sanctions against those who breach the norm.

By the age of sixteen, expectations have been communicated to the pupil. They are translated into predictions of success or failure, reward or punishment. They intermesh with parental influence. Let us be clear that it is not the absence or presence of parental interest that is crucial, but the way interest is expressed. If a climate of blame and punishment has developed or the student believes that whatever his effort his parent will never be satisfied, performance will deteriorate, unless he enjoys building identity by opposition. Boys have a special aversion to the negatively expressed concern of their fathers. Students from good homes effectively implement the most painful punishment for parents who flout their individuality, i.e., they fail in school, and withdraw from their parents.

The motive to achieve is subjective and learned. Perceptions of the probability of success, and the incentive value of success, have to be considered by the investigating tutor. Note that it is not one way – if success is too easily obtainable, there is nothing in which to take pride.

3 *A strategy*
  a Investigation of underfunctioning is not easy. There are no set recipes, therefore the strategy outlined is not to be followed automatically.
  b Ask: Is the underfunctioning *general* or *specific*?

  If there is firm evidence that it is specific, the problem probably belongs to the subject department. There could be a specific disability or a failure in learning essential concepts underlying the underfunctioning.
  c If underfunctioning is general, assess general ability. The Heim AH2 or AH4 provide sound measures. But caution is necessary.

  The test must be administered according to the instructions. Rapport must be created between the tester and the pupil. Over-reliance must not be placed on a single test administered by a specific person in a particular context.
  d Ask: *i* When the underfunctioning began?
         ii How it began? Suddenly, or over a relatively long period of time?

  Beware the tendency to find a single cause, because of the need to allocate meaning to behaviour. There is a possibility that extrinsic factors such as home circumstances played a part if there was a sudden change.
  e The next step towards diagnosis is collection of information which is structured by the following questions:
    a In what situations is the underfunctioning especially severe? e.g., practical, computational, etc.
    b In what situations does the student do relatively well?
    c What are his/her friends' values? Is there evidence of a pay-off for underfunctioning, e.g. acceptance by a group of friends?
    d Does the student lack skills, e.g. verbal or spatial?

  Follow this by collection of information again from teachers and lecturers about:
    a Reactions to frustration.
    b Response to challenge. Is the student motivated by fear of failure?

    c Beliefs about the nature of success, and the tendency to blame others for failures.

Then:
    a Discuss with the student his predictions of success and the future, especially career plans. It is likely that the pupil will be in a state of 'drift'.
    b Use some instrument such as:
       i The Lewis Counselling Inventory (NFER);
      ii The Aberdeen Academic Motivation Inventory (Entwistle N., British Journal Educational Psychology, Vol. 38, p.181, 1968).
    c Gather information from colleagues about the student's tendency to be prone to anxiety. Look for evidence of examination or test anxiety.
    d Assess study skills with a checklist (see p. 38). Pay special attention to listening and reading skills.

A warning and a reassurance

The warning – the high achiever has a strong preference for the intermediate level of difficulty in tasks. But this is associated with knowledge about his efforts and abilities. Those who have a strong desire to achieve like to get feedback about themselves and their performance. Low self-awareness may be associated with underfunctioning. Questioning may evoke the response, 'Don't know'. The use of checklists allows a dialogue to begin.

The reassurance – a structured case conference of those who teach the underfunctioning student will usually produce much of the information needed.

f Prescription.
    i Discuss the problems with the student. Arrange them in order of difficulty. Principles of treatment are:
       a Graduation.
       b Setting short-term goals.
    These two principles help structure an amorphous situation, and make change appear possible. Begin with the easiest elements, i.e., where the pupil predicts the greatest likelihood of change.
    ii Provide help with study skills. Introduce the pupil to diagrams and other methods of processing information (see Hamblin, 1981). If possible, include him in a special group or let him work with a friend. Supportive help from a peer

works well, providing the peer is well chosen and is involved in the task.

iii It is useful to have a set of tapes on study skills which the underfunctioning pupil can consult. Tutors will need such back-up material.

iv For economy of effort the tutor should offer group counselling to underfunctioning pupils. Attitude change and the acquisition of skills can be induced more readily in this setting, which avoids the resistance and negative expectations associated with the individual interview. Group counselling, to be effective, must be backed by individual targets and support. Group programmes will tackle the following areas, although other elements may enter:
  - predictions and their function in success or failure;
  - defences against learning;
  - the skills of study;
  - reactions to frustration;
  - fear of loss of face;
  - peer pressures;
  - developmental issues – autonomy, etc.

v The individual programme can be prescribed only to suit a specific case or group. Subject teachers and lecturers should be involved, and security be provided for the pupil by a unified approach. The role of the tutor is that of a mobiliser of resources and a monitor of progress.

vi Methods should build up a sense of competence. Behind the underfunctioning may lie a sense of powerlessness. Students should be involved in planning their group guidance programme of study skills and other activities. This can be done in sub-groups within the group counselling situation.

vii Parents may have played a part in creating the situation. This must be explored, and sometimes parents will need support to change their interaction with the pupil. Excessive criticism, pressure to achieve what is beyond the capacity of the pupil, or negative comparisons with an elder brother or sister may have to be dealt with. Parents are often uneasily aware that they have become trapped in a self-defeating pattern of interaction, but need help to escape from it.

Nothing will work if the teaching methods are inappropriate, the curriculum is irrelevant and the ethos of the institution is negative. Guidance cannot compensate for these inadequacies.

	STUDY DIFFICULTIES: A BRIEF CHECK LIST	Like me	Not like me
1	Get bored quickly in lessons.	☐	☐
2	Don't know how to make good notes.	☐	☐
3	Worry about making mistakes.	☐	☐
4	Can't take in what some teachers say.	☐	☐
5	Read rather slowly.	☐	☐
6	If I meet a difficult bit when reading, I skip over it.	☐	☐
7	Find it hard to remember what I have read.	☐	☐
8	Rarely test myself when I have finished reading.	☐	☐
9	Often forget things I need to bring to school.	☐	☐
10	Can't make my books look neat and attractive.	☐	☐
11	Teachers say I go off target and don't put down the key points in essays.	☐	☐
12	Never seem to have enough time to finish an essay.	☐	☐
13	Find it difficult to get started on my homework at night.	☐	☐
14	Put off revising for examinations.	☐	☐
15	Don't make a revision timetable. I revise when I feel like it.	☐	☐
16	Often don't answer examination questions in the way the teachers want.	☐	☐

Notes for the counsellor
This is not a test. It merely helps the student discuss study difficulties. Any 'Like me' endorsements provide an opening for counselling.

Students could follow this up with a diagnostic essay, *The Kind of Learner I am*. Get them to write it in the third person: 'John is the kind of learner who - - -' or 'John's strengths as a learner are - - -'

Case histories

The earlier discussion is now given shape by two case histories which raise questions for the reader. They will also make excellent material for a tutor in-service training group. One history deals with the negative impact of comparisons on a student, the other with more subtle erosion of identity.

> *Decision-making Exercise*
> Paul – aged 16 years

The general background

Paul is an able boy. He is particularly excellent in the field of verbal reasoning, but his work in mathematics and science is also good. He is well built and rather tall for his age, but he has become round-shouldered during the last year. Paul suffers from adolescent acne and is very self-conscious about it.

During the last six months his work has diminished in quantity and deteriorated in quality, although it is still up to the average of his tutor group, which is composed of fairly good students. This deterioration is a subtle one, consisting of a loss of originality and sparkle. The quality of his work is best summed up as 'inert' or showing 'passive compliance' with demands. His teachers still think well of him but are worried about his loss of liveliness and his tendency to reproduce mechanically what he has read or has been taught. He took seven O-levels and reached reasonable levels in them.

His home background is excellent, both parents being well educated and successful. He has an older brother who gained a first-class honours degree in sociology and is now doing research. His sister is three years older than Paul and is doing well at university.

Paul's story

You have seen him. Immediately you recognise that he is an extremely worried boy, but you are surprised to find that he is also a violently angry boy under the polite veneer.

He is worried because:
  i   he feels he will almost certainly fail his A-levels;
  ii he is spending three hours every evening on revision and homework and quite a lot of the weekend – yet he cannot remember what he reads and feels he has learned nothing;
  iii he feels he is going to disappoint both his parents and his teachers and he wants to please them;

iv he feels ugly, helpless and devalued.

He is angry because:
i he is always being compared with his brother and sister, who are held up to him as models whom he should emulate;
ii he feels nobody values him for himself but only as a reflection of the brother and sister;
iii he dislikes himself for not having the moral courage to reject this comparison process, and especially for not having the strength to drop out of school 'to be himself'.

Your problem

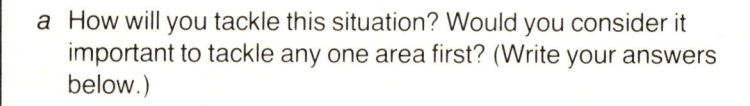

---

a How will you tackle this situation? Would you consider it important to tackle any one area first? (Write your answers below.)

---

b What will you do to help Paul cope with the learning and retention problem?

---

c How will you cope with the negative effects of the apparently helpful system of expectations and comparison which have been built up?

---

d Is there any way of dealing with Paul's body image that would help him?

A Fragment of a Case Study for Discussion
Eric – or 'I only tried to help'

Basic information
Eric was 16 when first seen by the counsellor and was due to repeat

his O-levels in six months' time. He was of good appearance, his ability was more than adequate, his powers of communication were good. He wanted to succeed, but his high level of aspiration was accompanied by a lack of belief in his own ability and a growing sense of failure. Eric related this to his poor performance in the internal examinations at the beginning of the fifth year, and he had shown signs of deterioration in his school work for at least four terms. The reader should be clear that no crude or direct causal relationship is being postulated between the attitudes which have been described and his poor performance. It was speculated, however, that:

a they might be interacting and strengthening each other, i.e., *each one in turn could be both cause and effect*;

b that attitudes and performance could both be the result of some other, as yet unknown, factor.

Eric was popular with his peers and his teachers found him pleasant and co-operative. He was good at sport, interested in music and obviously led a full and satisfying life.

His parents were supportive, allowing him freedom and encouraging his hobbies and activities. Eric received warmth, affection and appreciation from intelligent and concerned parents, yet he was beginning to underfunction and certainly displayed real anxiety. His father was an able and successful schoolmaster holding a senior post in his school and enjoying his work. (He did not work in his son's school.) Deep bonds of affection existed between son and both parents, and the marriage was stable and happy.

The counsellor was faced with the task of understanding why this boy, who appeared to have everything in his favour, was reacting in this way. *Note the tentative assumption that the problem behaviour was a response*, rather than some deep-seated maladjustment or obscure personality difficulty. The counsellor was therefore applying the law of parsimony to his work.

The crucial interview
The relationship was established when the following emerged. Eric suddenly said he was 'fed up with his father'. His father closely checked his assignments and questioned him about them. In his desire to help, his father taught him. Eric focused on two themes.

i His work was never good enough – there was always something which his father said could be improved. He felt that, however well he did it, he was expected to do better. There was no end to this process.

ii He felt even more strongly that his work was not his own but his father's, and that this was intolerable.

After elaboration of these points, Eric produced more deep feelings.
 i He felt that his father did not understand that he thought in a different way. A foreign style of thinking was being imposed on him.
 ii This led him to adopt unprofitable strategies in his work – the most marked being that of trying to learn everything off by heart. He then said that this meant he went into exams with no ideas of his own, and feeling unable to remember the ones which did not belong to him.

Much more developed in this interview, but this is sufficient for the case study. First, answer the following questions.

1 a Is there a link between this case and the adolescent's crisis of identity?
  ....
  b If so, what is it?
  ....

2 Eric showed anxiety about being disloyal to his father. He said, 'He's still my father – there are a lot of great things about him.'
  a How do you think the father reacted when he was approached?
  ....
  b How would you approach the father?
  ....

3 How would you deal with this boy's anxiety?
  ....

4 How would you continue with this case?
  ....

5 a What especially interests you about Eric's difficulties?
  ....
  b Why?
  ....

A note on the family

Guidance does not ask the tutor to become a 'diluted social worker'. We must not usurp the functions of the professional social worker, who is well trained and able to deal with the complications of distorted roles and interaction within the home. We can, however, ask and attempt to answer relevant professional questions.
  1 What has the student learned within the home, which impinges directly on his or her performance at school or college?
  2 Has he learned to predict failure?
  3 Has he learned to react automatically to authority or threat by aggression?
  4 Has he learned to take up certain roles in groups of peers?

5 Has he developed the tactic of meeting challenge by evasion?

Students will provide evidence about the nature of control at home. Some parents rely on positional control, which is illustrated by the following:

Child Why should I do it?

Parent Why? Because I'm your father, that's why!

Students from such homes may display two tendencies. The first extreme is that of over-dependence accompanied by a need for structure which amounts to being told exactly what to do. They reject responsibility for themselves and rely on the paternalistic tutor. To adopt a quasi-parental role towards them is to inhibit growth. The other extreme is that of vigilance against any hint of paternalism and positional control. Defensiveness leads them to misinterpret the tutor's intention, or to reject badly needed help in order to maintain an illusory independence. Enough has been said to alert the tutor to the need to keep from role boundaries and recognise the limitations of guidance. The most we can do in relation to family difficulties is help the student react in less costly ways if the student requests our help.

3: Group guidance and counselling

Summary points

> 1 Clear objectives and firm structure are essential in group guidance. Effort is best directed towards the modification of current behaviours, and the acquisition of necessary ones. It is desirable to involve students in planning the content of sessions.
> 2 Style of leadership is explored. Productive leadership in group counselling is linked with appropriate expression of concern, the ability to help students understand the meaning of events, and the capacity to manage guidance sessions.
> 3 The use of simulation, games, social modelling theory and a variant of fixed role therapy is discussed and illustrated. Cautions are expressed about over-reliance on role play, and the dangers inherent in this technique are examined.
> 4 The link between other forms of curriculum development and the construction of guidance modules is acknowledged.

A Reminder

Counselling is seen as an activity pursued as part of guidance. In practice, it is likely that no distinction will be made. The traditional distinction has been that guidance is directive and counselling non-directive. In *The Teacher and Counselling* (1974) I point out that ostensibly non-directive counselling can sometimes include an unintended and unrecognised process of non-verbal reinforcement. Latent processes are as relevant as the manifest. What is important is the student's sense of mastery and his active attempts to pursue his self-set goals.

The need for negotiation and student involvement in guidance was stressed in Chapter 1. Tutors involved in guidance should also negotiate as a group, sharing ideas and exploring the methodological problems. This is helpful in individual guidance, but fundamental for the development of sound group guidance in a particular institution. Acceptance of the fact that the ethos of the school or college, educational methods and the history of innovations determine the fate of innovations is too easily neglected. What works in one school or college will not work in another. What can be achieved in one institution can be achieved in another by a different route.

Limits of group guidance
We must beware of making extravagant claims for group guidance. Expression of commitment to a path of action and the practice of skills in the presence of peers certainly increase the likelihood that the student will carry out his intentions in other areas of his life. It would not, however, be common sense to assume that all group experiences are therapeutic or educative. Scapegoating, negative labelling and attack have marked many group experiences – indeed, students spend a great deal of time worrying about such things. Self-confidence can be eroded as well as enhanced through group experience. Superficially attractive forms of group guidance may be futile because they provide a version of the entertainment found in parlour games.

It can be argued that group counselling can sometimes demonstrate man's talent for distorting and vulgarising his own reality. Contradictory processes are involved: courting spontaneity by artifice; attempting to achieve genuineness by contrivance; engineering autonomy by group processes and pressures. These criticisms are relevant to only a few approaches, but such distortions do enter group guidance if we are not alert.

Roles are tried on in exaggerated ways in adolescence, although the larger-than-life postures conceal inner doubt. 16 - 19 year olds look at their parents, detecting a weary resignation or quiet despair under the flurry of parental activity. They then question the validity of their own aims. Some feel, in the poignant words of graffiti, 'We are the people our parents warned us against'. Distrust marks reactions to school and college, e.g., 'What are they trying to do to me?' The response to the belief that identities have been imposed on them is to generate an artificial self or façade to allow coping. The personal cost of this is high.

Vulnerability creates ambivalence. Group guidance which encourages premature self-exposure or 'psychic strip-tease' should be rejected by the responsible tutor. Most of us would accept this viewpoint. We may not notice, however, that group activities may strengthen adherence to the norms of the group, which, in turn, imposes on some groups a norm of mediocrity. Critical thought is essential. Quicke (1978), analysing Rogers's client-centred approach to counselling, claims that it reduces to endorsement of the personal *status quo* under the guise of self-acceptance. If this occurs, I consider it a misuse of Rogers's theory, but it does show that the apparently forward-looking can conceal unintended ties to a state of no change.

An old distinction is that between task orientation and relationship orientation. We could assume that group guidance and counselling should improve the quality of the student's relationships. Guidance cannot be conducted in a vacuum. Tasks have to be set and skills acquired. A balance between task and relationship orientation has to be achieved which suits a specific group. There is no recipe which caters for all group situations. At all costs, the normative fallacy (Reddin, 1970) which says there is one right balance of task and relationship orientation for all groups should be avoided. Adaptation to the group must occur. Even within the same institution groups will need different degrees of structure and emphasis in the activities.

Study skills, social skills and decision-making pitched at an appropriate level are topics suited to group guidance. Change of behaviour and the acquisition of new ways of coping form the focus of group guidance. This makes the *structure* of group guidance vital. Not only must it be constructive, but it must be seen as such by students.

The structure of group guidance

1 The purpose, objectives and proposed number of sessions must be explained *individually* to each student. This ensures accurate orientation to the task, allows negotiation and eliminates misconceptions.
2 Each session should:
- include planned activities with clear objectives which are explained to the students;
- end with a summary activity which shows what has been learned, and reinforces its applications;
- use some of the following methods:
   partner work;
   small group work;
   behaviour modification activities such as planning, working out strategies for coping, etc;
   decision-making;
   simple games and simulations.

A BASIC PRINCIPLE
USE PEER COUNSELLING TO THE FULL.
SET A FRIEND TO WORK WITH A FRIEND.

Group counselling offers an opportunity to break into the inertia or resistance of the peer group through mutual help. Let me stress that the methods used must fit the skills and confidence of the tutor. The principle of graduation applies to the tutor. There is no point in adopting a programme without understanding the implications. Beginning with what is possible prevents us from wandering into disaster. Barriers and hazards will appear that have to be overcome. If we do well what is within our scope we can gradually extend our techniques, and build up a productive individual style of guidance.

Group counselling is best seen as a carefully controlled learning process, providing knowledge and skills. It differs from other forms of learning only because the subject and object of the learning are identical, i.e., the learner is learning about himself in important ways. The tutor is not creating a climate in which revelations about family or past history have to be made. Concern is with current behaviours, their control, modification and consequences. If students are victims of their past, their present behaviour is shaped by it. Our objective is to help the student live life more effectively now, looking to the future constructively.

Concern with immediate behaviours makes the work of Rotter *et al* (1972), who stress learning, very relevant to group guidance. Their Social Learning Theory highlights expectations, preferences for taking up a particular role in a group and the rewards sought by the individual. Habitual roles and reactions in groups where an authority figure is present also operate in group guidance sessions, when the stances taken towards peers are also visible. Tutors note these things, and then help students to consider or change them.

Typical questions asked by the tutor

1. What roles has this student taken up?
2. Does he passively acquiesce in my suggestions without real intention to act on them?
3. Does he rely on peers to make up his mind for him, showing undue sensitivity to approbation or blame from peers?
4. Is he suspicious of adults?
5. Does he try to lead, but fail because he alienates others by aggression or insensitivity?

Mechanisms operate in group counselling through which students divert attention from themselves by questioning others. Clowning roles prevent people from looking too closely, because the clown is often likeable. The resident cynic who gains attention and power through discrediting others' motives or pouring cold water on enthusiasm has to be dealt with. The tutor will find it useful to develop a taxonomy of roles. Discussion with fellow tutors secures a greater profit from the exercise below.

Tutor activity

Work with a partner, if possible.

| List below the roles which you think may be a focus for your attention in group guidance sessions, e.g., trouble-maker or clown. | Make brief notes on:
i the reasons for paying attention to them;
ii the way in which you would intervene. |

Follow-up discussion, when this exercise is part of preparation of a group of tutors for group counselling or guidance, should focus on the ways in which students cope with tension and challenge, collude with others when being disruptive, or achieve pay-offs for their behaviour. Passive resistance is more difficult to cope with than active, because a class can force a teacher to nag or hector, and then ignore him because of the reaction they have provoked. Detection of implicit bargains negotiated with teachers is salient in good group guidance, e.g., 'If you don't bother me too much, I won't bother you!' Mechanisms such as avoidance of challenge, assumption of false superiority through denigration of others are germane to group guidance. In their own way, tutors should detect and then examine the function of such behaviour. Students will have to be confronted constructively with what they do if they are to gain control of their lives. Without the tutor stimulating insight into their patterns of behaviour change is unlikely.

Leadership

Tutors cannot abdicate their responsibility for critical scrutiny of what happens in guidance sessions. Alertness to the possibility of damage and the ability to intervene are key skills. Some groups need more structure and control than others, as much because threat and anxiety are present in the situation as from aggressive and disruptive tendencies in the students. Parsons and Bales (1953) detect two forms of leadership. Task leadership is associated with organising the attack on the problems of the group. Social-emotional leadership is the pouring of oil on troubled waters after friction has occurred. Cohesion is thus restored. Balance is essential. Too little task orientation brings danger of drift. Too strong an emphasis on social and emotional leadership and stagnation occurs: too little, and unresolved tensions split the group and conflict assumes more importance than task achievement. The perceptive analysis of group leadership by Lieberman *et al* (1973) has helped me to construct the outline below.

The major orientation of the group leader

1 *Stimulation of emotions*
The leader creates a group climate in which emotions are stimulated and expressed. He acts as a model expressing warmth, dependability, etc. He constantly calls assumptions into question, challenging through confrontation. He becomes the focus for the feelings of members of the group.

2 *Concern*
This orientation allows the expression of warmth. The hallmark is deep concern, acceptance and genuine regard for group members.

3 *Helping members understand events*
The tutor attempts to explain what is happening between individuals or within the group. The climate of the group and the approach to tasks is carefully scrutinised. Members are encouraged to think about events.

4 *Structure and management*
Rules and limits are clearly established. The use of time and the introduction of tasks are carefully managed.
Actions tend to be controlled.

All these orientations enter into group leadership in practice. The mixture will differ with the tutor and the composition and purpose of the group. Lieberman *et al* provide some evidence that *concern* and *helping understanding* are key elements in successful group counselling. Orientations imply behaviour.

> **Leader behaviour**
>
> 1 *Behaviours which evoke student responses*
>   These include questioning, reflecting back (described in Chapter 2), challenge, invitations to speak, confrontation, and, least effective, exhortation.
> 2 *Behaviours which explain what is happening*
>   Clarification, giving a summary, comparisons and contrasts, invitations to students to seek feedback, and providing a plan for change fall into this area.
> 3 *Supportive behaviours*
>   Support, praise and encouragement.
> 4 *Management behaviours*
>   Pacing, setting time limits, introducing and controlling activities and interrupting certain behaviours.

This catalogue is only of use when it becomes a basis for tutor self-evaluation. Questions should be raised, e.g. 'Do I give enough explanation?'; 'Do I give it without being dogmatic?'; or 'Have I the ability to express concern constructively?'

Objectives
In relation to the above, objectives must not only be clear in the mind of the tutor, but they must be justified to the students. They then know the criteria for success in the group, and can assess their own progress. Structure is not rigidity. Objectives can be clarified or modified as the group develops. Members should be involved in the revision of goals and selection of activities. Tutors might now try this exercise:

> **Trainer activity**
>
> Work out how you would explain to pupils the objectives of:
> a a group dealing with disruptive behaviour in class;
> b sessions which modify attitudes to learning and develop the skills of study;
> c group-counselling sessions which help pupils with careers decisions;
> d a programme which hopes to correct timidity and social anxiety in withdrawn pupils, and to teach the assertive behaviours.

It will be illuminating if explanations are tape-recorded and then examined critically from the standpoint of the students.

Games and simulations

Games! The word arouses confused feelings. Ideas of chance, dice and counters may float across our minds. Complicated matrices of possible courses of action and sophisticated mathematical analyses are another more intimidating aspect of games theory. Fortunately, for guidance purposes a game simply presents its players with a situation to which they must respond by evaluating possibilities, selecting a course of action and looking at the consequences of implementing it. A fuller description can be found in Hamblin (1974). Games provide vicarious experience of making decisions and assessing costs of a line of action. Students learn:

1 about interaction in social situations where prestige, assessment and embarrassment are important factors;
2 to anticipate the reactions of others, assessing the impact of their actions on people;
3 to scan and consider ways of mounting an effective attack on a problem;
4 to develop the skills of planning.

The basic principles are simplicity and relevance. We should decide what is to be learned, e.g., *specific* aspects of negotiation, co-operation, decision-making or ways of reacting. The example of a game originally constructed by a small group of my students may help. I have modified it in various ways.

Jobbo : A game for careers guidance

1 Each player has a small board of thin manilla card covered with self-adhesive film. (This allows us to make as many boards as we wish, because thin manilla 205mm x 250mm card will go through a spirit duplicator.)
The board is laid out in this way:

A Qualifications	B Personality qualities that will be useful	C Skills that are necessary

1 Small duplicated cards cover job title, qualifications, personality qualities and skills.
2 The game is played in groups of four. One of the four is a peer judge who will assess the validity of the bargaining that will occur.
3 A job title is selected by the three who have boards and placed in position.
4 Three piles of small cards are put in the middle covering the sub-headings on the boards. The piles containing B and C cover a far wider range of personality qualities and skills than are relevant.
5 Players in turn pick up a card from each pile and place it on their boards.
6 At the end of each round, if they feel the card is irrelevant they can bargain with another player. They explain why the personality, quality or skill they have is more suitable for the other person's board, and why they need his card for their board. The peer judge then makes a decision as to the fairness of the exchange.
7 If there is no exchange, and the card is obviously irrelevant it has to be put on one side.
8 When the boards are full, students discuss their occupation, checking how accurate other players feel their perceptions are.
N.B. The game is intended to stimulate thinking about occupations. The tutor will examine one board in depth in a constructive way, drawing attention to factors such as occupational stereotypes.

Tutors will find many helpful activities in the various Schools Council Projects on Careers Education and Guidance, Moral Education, Social Education and the Humanities. The rich legacy of those innovatory programmes can be put to use with profit.

Simulations

A simulation is an attempt to replicate the key issues or factors of important situations. It never completely reflects the complexity of real life, but is the equivalent of a model which highlights certain details. Many of the simulations used by the tutor would be concerned with social processes, bargaining, coping with criticism, peer pressures or leadership. A simple example will make this clear.

Preparation for work

> *At the cleaners – Script of tape-recording.*

Part 1

Door slams.

Kathy Gosh – that's the third time this week I've had a row from the boss. I'd better watch it – he's really gunning for me now. My boy-friend Sid, though – he's working in the butcher's down the road and he gets on great with his boss. Lucky him.

Part 2

Door opens.

Kathy Yes?
Customer I left a suit of my husband's in to be cleaned last week – it should be ready today.
Kathy Where's your ticket?
Customer Oh, I haven't got it – it's in my other bag. The suit's got grey checks, so you'll find it all right.
Kathy Look, there's a notice up there. We can't give you anything without a ticket.
Customer Now, don't be awkward. My husband needs that suit tonight. It won't be hard to find it.
Kathy Now – look. I can't - - -
Customer What a fuss over a ticket. Go and call the manager. I'd better talk to somebody sensible.
Kathy Okay – I'll get him.

Part 3

Kathy Trust me to get an old bag like her. Mr Brown said she could have the suit so I'd better look sharp and get it. Grey checks . . . that's what she said.
Here it is – hey, wait a minute. What's that big brown mark on the sleeve? It looks as though something's gone wrong with one of the machines. Grief! This will cause a fuss. Mr Brown's gone out, thank goodness. What'll I do? Just fold it up and pretend it's all right or tell her something's gone wrong?

Part 4

Kathy What a morning! That old bag insisted on checking the suit and she nearly blew her lid when she saw the stain.

	She says it's got to be fixed and she'll be back at five for it.
	Jim, look at this mess. What have you been playing at – working the machines with your eyes shut?
	What do you bet there are lots more clothes like this?
Jim	Hey, let me see that suit, Kathy. Gosh, it is a mess. When was it done?
Kathy	Yesterday, I suppose.
Jim	Oh . . . I'm for it now.
Kathy	What's the fuss?
Jim	Yesterday afternoon – you and Mr Brown were out – well, I nipped out to the chemist's to get a prescription for me mum. I left young Robert in here – I knew there'd be hardly anyone in. I bet he's been at the pressing machine. He knows he's not to use it without me there to watch him.
Kathy	Old Brown will flip his lid if he hears about this. You know what he's like.
Jim	Kathy, he's not as bad as all that – you just don't like him. Mind you, he'll give me a big row if he finds I left the shop. If the customer comes back and wants to see him you could tell her he's not in. We'll get the suit fixed up.
Kathy	Now hang on, Jim. I'm not getting into trouble for you.
Jim	Come on, just this once.
Kathy	You can tell him it's Robert's fault. Robert won't dare say anything – he's scared of the boss.
Jim	You don't like young Robert, you're always getting at him. I can't let him take the blame. I shouldn't have left him on his own. What a botch-up! How am I going to get out of this one?

Students would then explore the following questions:

Part 1

What do you think Kathy might have done to get into trouble with the boss? Can you think of *three* things?

Kathy says her boy-friend is lucky to get on with his boss. Is he just lucky?

If you think it's not just luck, put down what you think Sid might be doing to please his boss.

Part 2

Do you think Kathy treated this customer the right way? Give reasons for your answer.

Part 3

What do you think Kathy should do with the suit? Should she pretend there is no stain?

Part 4

When the customer comes in to get the suit, should Kathy do as Jim has asked and pretend Mr Brown is out?
Write down why you have given this answer.
Should Jim pretend *he* made a mistake with the pressing machine? What do you think?
Kathy said that Jim should blame Robert. Is that a good idea?
Should Jim go and admit to Mr Brown what happened?
If Jim does that, what do you think Mr Brown might say to him?
Should young Robert get any of the blame?
All this happened because Jim left the shop. What should he have done?
After listening to this tape, what sort of person do you think Jim might be?
After listening to this tape, what sort of person do you think Kathy might be?

The script is taped, therefore it can be part of a resources bank of materials from which tutors can draw. Decision-making exercises are simple and productive. For effective learning the tutor should concentrate on one aspect only. The simple diagram on page 56 will act as an initial guide to students. Note that it leaves out the important issue of level of risk.

How decisions are made

Making a decision is not always as simple as it may seem. We actually go through a number of stages, although we may not be aware of this at the time.

A simple decision-making exercise is given as a guide.

Drive or Walk

1 *Objectives*
To help students evaluate the acceptable level of risk in a situation where conventional stereotypes may be at work. The tutor may also draw attention to the credibility of the source of a message if he desires.

Stage 1

What are you deciding?

Think about

a What you want to achieve.
b What will happen without a decision.
c How *you* make a decision. Are you:
   Impulsive?
   Easily influenced by others?
   Someone who looks for alternatives?

Stage 2

What information do you need?

Where can you obtain it?   What alternative does it suggest?

Stage 3

How do you use the information?

Consider

a Its relevance to what you want to do.
b Its source and accuracy.
c The effects of rejecting alternatives.

Stage 4

What do you decide?

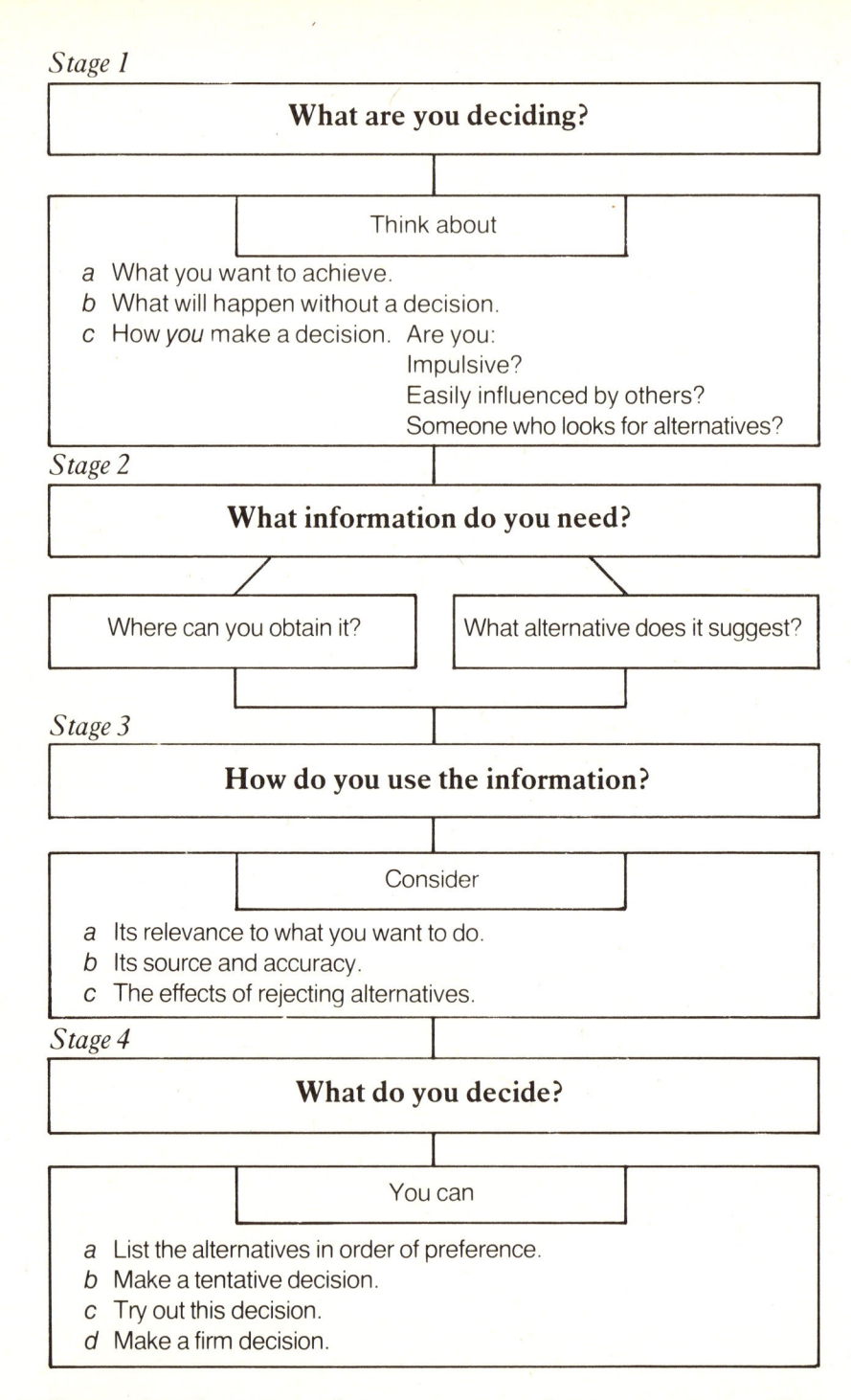

You can

a List the alternatives in order of preference.
b Make a tentative decision.
c Try out this decision.
d Make a firm decision.

Remember that at any time you may need to return to an earlier stage.

2 *Situation*
   Bill has brought his three friends to a party, in his father's car which he borrowed with permission. By the end of the evening two of them have decided to go off with friends. Bill has had more to drink than the law allows the driver. Mike, who is reserved and the sort of person people ignore, says they ought to leave the car and walk home. Bill's reply is that Mike worries too much, and that there is no danger as they have only three miles to go along a fairly quiet road.
   What do you think he ought to do?
3 *Activity*
   In groups of three or four, argue about the situation and come to a decision. Then ask how much part was played in your decision by:
   a prudence and the possible consequences;
   b protection of your toughness and masculinity;
   c concern for other people;
   d the credibility of Mike as a source of influence.

Other methods

The use of social modelling

The section on behaviour change in Chapter 2 underlined the fact that students can be limited in their knowledge of behaviour. The following script has been used to teach a productive way of coping with a difficult situation.

WAS HE ACCUSED?

The situation
You work in a warehouse which deals with sports clothing and accessories. The goods are very attractive, selling well, and as soon as new goods come in they are despatched. Pressures on staff are high because of the success of this relatively new firm. The checking of stock and the control of workers is a little erratic, perhaps inefficient. Things tend to get mislaid and tempers fray. There has also been some suspicion that there is a small amount of pilfering, but this is uncertain.

Tapescript 1
   Foreman   Jim, have you seen a pile of those new X07 terylene and cotton tracksuits?

Jim	Can't remember them coming my way. Are you sure they haven't gone out? A big consignment of them went off to Brown's, North London, last week.
Foreman	Damn! Now we're in trouble. I've just had the boss on my back about the disappearance of stuff. He's getting fed up. Do you know anything about it?
Jim	What do you mean? Are you accusing me or something? It's your job to see things don't go missing, not mine.
Foreman (somewhat angrily)	That's enough of that. I've put up with your lip before. If things are being lifted who's in the best position to get stuff out of the warehouse? Lads like you are always being sent out with small local parcels, and there's no check.
Jim (angry now)	Flipping Emma! I do believe you're accusing me. Are you?
Foreman	If the cap fits, you wear it! Stuff is going, and somebody's responsible.
Jim (shouting)	You bald-headed old bastard! If you did your work properly instead of spending half the day behind the stacks with Moira – she's quids in with you – it would be better for everybody. Does your missus know?
Foreman	Look lad, that's enough of your cheek. It's up to the office with you. You can say what you want up there, but I've had enough of you. Come on – get moving – Mr Young will sort you out.
Jim (almost berserk)	Push off, fat guts! I'll go in my own way. Stuff your crummy job.

> After this the group could discuss the likely outcomes. If Jim is dismissed, will it be because he did pilfer, or because he was insubordinate? Consideration of what would happen when he goes for another job then follows. Would a telephone call be made to the warehouse, and what would be said? If he remains in his job, how would he repair his working relation with the foreman? Examination of the reasons for Jim's responses, and the ease with which conflict escalates around such topics should occur.

Tapescript 2

Then the second part is played.

Foreman Jim, have you seen a pile of those new X07 terylene and cotton tracksuits?

Jim   Can't remember them coming my way. Are you sure they haven't gone out? A big consignment of them went off to Brown's North London, last week.

Foreman   Damn! Now we're in trouble. I've just had the boss on my back about the disappearance of stuff. He's getting fed up. Do you know anything about it?

Jim   Let me think. Some stuff came in on Friday, but I didn't have time to look at it. It's over there. (Sounds of rummaging.) No, it's not the tracksuits.

Foreman   Well, I'm getting a bit worried. I've just had the boss on my back about things going missing, as I said. Somebody must know something.

Jim   Well, I suppose it's a bit rough having to carry the can for it. I'd never grass on me mates anyway, but they're straight. I wouldn't touch anything – I want my job. The old man's lost his, and I can see what it's like.

Foreman   Okay, Jim. But have you got any ideas about these blanketty X07 tracksuits?

Jim   Look, why don't we have another check?
(Vague rustlings and mutters.)
Here's the original invoice. What't this? 'P.T.O.' Hey, look – 'X07 to follow' – the nuts put it on the back of the invoice!

Foreman   That stupid lot. Next they'll send them from Rochdale here via Hong Kong. I'll phone them and see what they're playing at. Thanks, mate.

The guidance group can then discuss the different outcome. The moods and idiosyncracies of immediate supervision at one's workplace should be anticipated. Futility of personal abuse, and the need to change an antagonistic situation into a cooperative one without debasing oneself could come to the fore profitably.

Fixed role therapy
Social modelling theory as adopted above gives students a chance to compare two ways of behaving in the same situation. Kelly's (1955) fixed role approach can be employed in a modified form. A narrative is constructed, and then taped or duplicated. It describes someone coping with a problem or topic central to the group counselling. Five or six minutes is long enough for a tape. It is played, and then students are asked to make notes as they listen again, criticising the strategies described, finding better ways of doing it, and beginning to

work out their own way of coping. The tape functions as a point of departure. Not so obvious is the way the tape exploits the students' tendency to get identity by opposition. Many young people resent being told how to do something, taking a position of indifference or weary resignation. Thrusting them into a critical position disrupts their expectations.

The ideas of *graduation* and *experimentation* are also used. The students are encouraged to work out the first steps they would take, and arrange them in a hierarchy of difficulty. They then agree to try out the first step for three days and report back in the group sessions – it is a kind of experiment. Pressure is therefore avoided, actually making success more likely. If failure occurs, the tutor can use it as an opportunity for learning. An outline script might take this form:

Script: Coping with the pressures of examinations
Julie was a conscientious worker and prepared diligently for her examinations. She knew her trouble was that she tended to react badly. When her parents enquired how she reacted, she said she was never sure if she was going to get a tight feeling like an over-wound clock spring or whether she was going to drop to bits. Sometimes, she said – and they felt it was true – both happened simultaneously. After a panic the week before the examination Julie vowed she'd do something about the way she coped.

Her first step was to make a plan. What would be her revision strategies during this last week? She made a balance sheet between strong and weak subjects. Then she looked at them from a different viewpoint. Which were the really important ones for her future plans? She thought it would be foolish to spend too much time on her weakest subjects – that would only depress her. Fortunately, none were vital to her planned career as a laboratory technician with a local firm. Her next step was an outline chart for the week which showed how often she would revise each subject. She also made very clear plans for tackling the three important subjects which were essential for her job.

Then it was the 'how' that had to be tackled. Julie enjoyed using diagrams as a way of dealing with key points. Her idea was to make a set of cards with a diagram on one side of the card and the keypoints set out as if they were newspaper headings on the other.

Fine! She almost relaxed. Then some nasty thoughts hit her. Last time she got worked up the night before her last exams began. Inside, her stomach was churning, she felt desperate, and when her mother said, 'Don't worry – you'll be all right', she nearly hit her. A hopeless feeling overcame her, so she tried to test herself by repeating out loud all the facts she could remember. That made it worse. What did she feel? Well, that she didn't know a thing and never would. 'No point in letting that happen again,' she said firmly to herself. So she decided this time to take the main topic cards she'd made. She would look at the diagrams and then make a new one without looking at the other. That would help her see how much she could get down on paper. She had tried this and it had seemed to work. Also she was quite clear she was going to bed by eleven o'clock. 'At least it won't be like last time when I stayed up to 3.30 a.m. for the last three nights. The bags under my eyes were down to my knees by the time I began the exam.' Julie laughed, but . . .

Breakfast! She was trying to slim a bit, and she usually dodged breakfast, especially when her dad greeted her with, 'Now, my girl, when I was your age I always had a good cooked breakfast.' Julie recalled how faint and empty she had felt last time in her morning exams around 11.30 a.m. She had slowed down, and then couldn't finish the last question. So she made up her mind to have orange juice and scrambled egg. Perhaps honey on her toast as well. She liked honey.

Next – she'd better read the paper more carefully this time. She had nearly kicked heself last time when afterwards she'd found two questions she could have answered better. Somehow she hadn't noticed. Two minutes spent scanning the paper might save her trouble. Then, 'What did that bloke say who came to talk about study skills? Of course, look at the verb, it tells you what to do. Oh, and I mustn't spend too much time on my first question like I did last time.'

Julie went downstairs. Dad was half asleep in the armchair as usual, supposed to be watching television. He grunted, and asked her how it was going. Julie told him what she was going to do, and he seemed pleased. 'Better than him moaning,' thought Julie. Dad spluttered into life. 'Hey, what was it that Miss Jones said when I saw her? Didn't she say you'd have done well if you had stayed on target?' Why couldn't he be honest? Julie knew he'd been saving that up since the parents' evening. This time she was ready, meaning what she said. 'Look, Dad, I've taught myself to make a plan quickly before I begin to write my answer.' That had been one of the good things they learned in the tutor group.

'Well, too bad if I don't do all right,' thought Julie. 'And I'm not having a post mortem once I've finished. I made myself on edge last time. I ran around, asking everybody how they did, and the only result was I felt horrible.'

Students can be encouraged to tape their own narrative, talking about themselves in the third person. Valuable discussion occurs, helping students to examine and clarify their learning strategies.

A note on role play

Role play is being brought into many guidance programmes. It is useful, but it is also a powerful and intimidating technique. In 1974 I cautioned that it could be used in an authoritarian manner to suggest 'the right answer'. This limits learning. Of necessity, it is a simplification of reality and could lead students to believe change is simpler than it is. Then, if they fail, they label themselves unable to change. Such misuse does not condemn a technique, but it does show the need for caution. Role play itself is a skill used to teach other skills. Therefore we need to introduce it gradually. Two or three minutes is enough if students are unused to it. Role play should help participants understand the standpoint of the other person. Hence both roles must be played to stimulate appreciation of the contrasts and disjunctions in perceptions of the same situation.

Careful and gradual introduction is necessary, using the advice of a drama specialist. All role play can be preceded by discussion which stimulates ideas in students, but also allows the tutor to detect reservations, dislike and anxiety. Post-play discussion is essential to allow the learning to be consolidated, and its application to the student's life elaborated.

People have very strong reactions to role play. Some find it intolerable. This feeling has to be respected. Certain roles may carry unintended threat for the student. To be involved in a role play which centres on something of which the student is ashamed is threatening, not therapeutic. Family roles have to be regarded with caution. To ask someone to play a family role after a bereavement would be a crass insensitivity that few would commit. But the trouble is that with this age group, to whom sympathy is often abhorrent, we may not know of the situation because they conceal it. Forcing someone into a role by sweeping objections aside is a contravention of the basic ethic of respect. If a role contains an element that is threatening for a student, or something that he denies exists in himself, the experience can be destructive. It could be therapeutic but the risk cannot be assessed. In the matter of role play – if in doubt, don't!

Structure and content

The optimum size of a guidance group is between nine and fifteen people. Fewer participants reduce the range of activities and interaction, whilst individuals feel watched or too visible. More than fifteen brings a danger of the group splitting into sub-groups. Then one has a single group in terms of physical space, but two or more groups psychologically. Cohesion is helped by giving the objectives, specifying how long the group will last, and the immediate involvement of members in activity.

Careful planning is critical in the first session when perceptions of the utility of the group are formed. Transactions between tutor and group and between student and student take shape, and are not easily modified in later sessions. A vigorous, stimulating and satisfying first group means a high probability of success. Initial activities should not be ambiguous if distrust is not to be aroused.

Work in small groups of three or four allows communication to develop. Membership of these sub-groups should vary to give more experience before longer lasting working groups are formed. To get the atmosphere necessary for good group guidance, students must be placed in a number of simple helping situations with one another. Planning an attack on a problem, achieving a solution to a problem, provide examples. The tutor should set out to facilitate the establishment of helping relationships between students as vigorously as possible. The modification of attitudes and behaviour is always more likely to be permanent when friends offer support for it.

In a session there should be movement between partner work, small group work, individual activity, and activities pursued by the total group. No set pattern exists, except that it seems productive to reintegrate the group at the end of session. The final seven to ten minutes reduce tensions if they have appeared, but also should be used by the tutor to clarify what has been learned and show students how to apply it. Students must end a guidance session with a sense of success and knowledge that learning has occurred. Young adults find it difficult to tolerate a sense of stagnation – not only must they be developing, but know this is so. The less able, in particular, need clear, concrete targets.

Later sessions should provide thought-provoking, constructive encounters with relevant problems. Analysis of problems and drawing up a plan for tackling them can be done through diagrams. Students often have a preference for visual and active forms of learning, which must be encouraged in the guidance group. Note the word 'encouraged'. It is counter-productive to impose any approach on them: it stifles spontaneity.

Good tutors seize on opportunities to help the student realise that he largely created the environmental contingencies of which he complains. They have to understand that nobody *has* to react to a problem or situation in a particular way – an important piece of learning often neglected in guidance. If the student learns to modify his behaviours and anticipate the reactions of others, he has more rewards from life. Put simply, if the student feels people 'pick on him, the guidance question is, 'What can you do to stop people picking on you?', i.e. by changing what he does. Frustration, loss of face and shame can be dealt with by looking at the situations in which they occur and treating them as suggested.

The final session should consolidate and recapitulate. Anticipation is again crucial. Students should be encouraged to look ahead and identify difficulties. They should work out ways of coping and identify sources of support. Realistic awareness of sources of tension coupled with strategies for dealing with them provide the sense of mastery that guidance should provide.

Content

Drawing up the content of a group guidance module differs little from other forms of curriculum development. Parker and Rubin (1966) argued that education had neglected *process* in learning. We have seen that our effort is directed towards active methods of acquisition of knowledge and its subsequent utilisation, i.e., process. Taba (1962) provides seven points which should underlie the planning of guidance modules.

1 Diagnosis of needs.
2 Formulation of objectives.
3 Selection of content.
4 Organisation of content.
5 Selection of learning experiences.
6 Organisation of learning experiences.
7 Determination of what to evaluate, and choosing appropriate forms of evaluation.

The initial emphasis by Taba on diagnosis of needs highlights the inadequacy of imposing wholesale a ready-made scheme. Bespoke tailoring is necessary. Taba's steps seem to interact rather than form a strict sequence. Tutors can consult and involve students in the two crucial elements of determination of content and selection of learning experiences. In this way the problems of accountability and acceptability are resolved. For expository purposes only the initial attempts at shaping the content of three short modules are set out below. The content was designed for particular groups and it was negotiated with participants.

Group guidance module: Aggressive behaviours

Topics
Dealing with frustration
Coping with loss of face.
The pay-offs from aggressiveness – new ways of achieving them.
Preventing aggression from escalating.
Things which trigger off trouble.
Coping with practical jokes or being laughed at maliciously.
Predictions about what will happen in certain situations.
Situations where things get out of hand.

Group guidance module: Study skills

Note-taking skills.
SQ3R for boosting reading efficiency.
Processing what has been learned – effective use of diagrams.
Revision strategies.
Self-diagnosis.
Coping with examination anxieties.
Self-management.

Group guidance module: Social skills

Initiating a conversation.
Joining in activities.
Listening as a social skill.
Embarrassment in social situations.
Coping with people in authority.
Using humour constructively.
Talking to different people for different purposes on the telephone.
Ways of joining an existing group of students.
Coping with unfamiliar situations where I don't know how to behave.

Such initial steps need to be developed in more detail and put into sequence. Then methods would be developed more precisely, e.g., would certain topics be best dealt with by decision-making exercises or games? Next, concrete situations are identified which will be acceptable to the students, or, even better, emanate from them. Finally, we specify what has to be learned in each exercise.

None of the above implies highly polished or complex simulations. But tutors must know what they are doing after consciously fitting the module to the needs of a specific group. The idea of piecemeal objectives (Davies, 1976), based on short modules and successive approximations, is to be commended. Grand plans can be a recipe for disaster in guidance. It is better for the tutor to apply his teaching skills to guidance. If activity is to be the mainspring of the sessions, the tutor's input must be concise and lucid. The 'listen to me' stage must be brief. Successful movement from individual to partner or small group work depends on clear instructions. Tutors should be meticulous about this, and about the timing of activities and the positive ending of the session which highlights the learning that has taken place, bearing in mind that students react strongly to initial experience in a session, and remember most clearly the closing activity.

Concluding note
Let me reiterate the factors which contribute to safety and a sense of purpose in group guidance.
1 Students should have the objectives explained clearly to them.
2 They should be involved in selection of the content of the sessions.
3 The number of sessions should be agreed on by tutor and students.
4 The fact that group guidance is a learning process of a practical kind should be stressed. Students should know it is intended to increase their active attempts at mastery of their environment and skills of self-management.

4: Adjustment to work, careers guidance and preparation for unemployment

Summary points

1. In the current economic situation, guidance programmes can usefully pay more attention to the social and psychological problems of adjustment in the first job. The emphasis is *not* on the transition from school to work. Activities should focus on stresses arising from common difficulties, which, if not dealt with competently, lead to young workers giving up a job, even when they know they are unlikely to get another.
2. The guidance programme should provide young people with the knowledge and skills essential for the maintenance of integrity, drive and self-respect during a period of unemployment. Self-defeating reactions or depression can occur, including new types of stress in family relationships, especially if the father is unemployed. Tutors should anticipate these possibilities, helping students understand them, and inoculating them against tensions, especially those stemming from devaluation of the unemployed.
3. Exchange relationships are the basis for social integration even in small-scale societies. If we ask, 'What have the unemployed to exchange?' the implications are clear. What are now called generic vocational skills should include a search for new, positive forms of exchange relationships with society, coupled with the development of *entrepreneurial* skills and initiative.
4. Long-term structural unemployment makes the broader forms of careers education more important. Preferences for certain job satisfactions, the relationship of work to life style, realistic examination of the fields in which job satisfaction could be found, and sharpening of work skills, are still essential. Exploration of new patterns of work, e.g., job sharing, may need more attention than they are given at the moment.

Why this title?
The three topics appear to make uneasy bed-fellows. They could be seen as antagonistic. Coping with the prospect of unemployment and the changes in the structure of industry is not defeatist. It would be unrealistic to ignore the consequences of technology.

Adjustment to work

Concern has been frequently expressed about the transition from school to work, e.g. Moor (1976), Rees and Smith (1980). A critical review by Clarke (1980) states that the assumption that entry into work is traumatic is unsupported. It may be true for a minority of individuals, but the majority of young people adapt well. Willis (1978) in his study of the transition showed how the 'lads' learned to cope with the irrelevance of school by creating diversions to lighten the boredom. Careers education of the traditional type has little relevance for them, yet they are being well trained within their sub-culture in the survival techniques necessary in routine, soul-destroying work. This has to be held in mind when we begin to talk about social skills. Personal experience taught the writer about the necessity of the minor ploys which make work bearable in occupations where hard physical work, heat and adjustment to machines eroded physical and social competence. Vocational skills may include examination of the ways in which workers manage these pressures. Evasiveness and lack of response to managerial blandishments have functions that may not be appreciated from the middle-class perspective. A salutary reminder that careers education cannot compensate for the experiences of the later years of compulsory schooling is helpful. Programmes of guidance may impose the irrelevant or what is relevant from the teacher standpoint. Does this mean we have nothing to offer?

Hayes (1971) illuminated the answer in his analysis of the way work is perceived before and after entry. Young workers realise that they did not know enough about the social and psychological stresses which arise in work, although they may have dealt with the physical features of their working environment. In my work I have found that there are a number of prototypical situations which cause young people to give up work – or toy with the idea – even when they realise they are scarcely likely to get another job. We are therefore concerned with adjustment *in* work rather than adjustment *to* work.

Authority is less predictable, especially at the level of chargehand or foreman. Immediate supervision in industry can be biased and crude. It is also a fact that, whilst the school urges students towards standards of excellence, the norm of the working group may be, 'Do as little as possible for as much as possible.' Every teacher knows, however, that this is also the case in school. Pupils who break the norm about the response to homework meet sanctions from their peer group. Some pupils can cope with this well, maintaining good relationships with peers whilst maintaining their own standards; others conform blindly or isolate themselves from the peer group. Most students work near home. Stresses exist which are peculiar to an occupation, perhaps to a particular valley. In looking at one very good firm I found the following unrecognised sources of stress among workers:

- lack of knowledge of the evaluations of supervisors during initial training;
- a conflict between full utilisation of the expensive raw material and the need to produce a required amount of the product, which was in high demand;
- communication difficulties between two workers on machines, where they could not see each other but still had to make joint decisions about trips to the cloakroom, etc;
- restriction of personal choice, e.g., sweets could not be eaten because the product absorbed smell.

Tutors should investigate such sources of stress, which will include the local labelling of girls who work in certain firms, physical violations, because the smell of fat, oils or other products used clings obstinately to hair and body despite washing. In one case, young people would work at a firm only as a last resort because the smell allowed them to be identified on the bus.

The module on work adjustment would usefully explore the following situations. It has been easiest to present them as decision-making exercises, followed by a number of possibilities for action. One should incorporate an *expedient* response, i.e., a short-term staving off of trouble, which in fact can bring serious consequences. Young people of reasonable intelligence and from solid backgrounds rely on rather childish mechanisms of this type, e.g., the 'tit for tat' response. They can be presented as playlets on tape or as paper and pencil activities.

Key principles in the module
1 Anticipation of stress or breakdown points.
2 Inoculation against impulsive reactions.
3 Inducing coping strategies.

Situation 1

Explanation

This would deal with the initiation which operates in many working groups. Young workers are still sent for the sky-hook, the tin of striped paint or the rubber-headed hammer on the first day of work, when they are confused. (The last example, of course, is not used as a joke in industries where sparks are not allowed.)

Situation

You are an apprentice, and you have been introduced immediately into a working group. A mass of details have been given to you and this, with the novelty of everything, makes you feel confused. Then the foreman comes up and says, 'Just nip down to Store A and get me a fallopian tube.' When you get there the storekeeper looks at you, asking about sizes, plastic or metal, flexible or rigid. His assistant is grinning in the rear, and suddenly you catch on – you've been had! Worst of all, on your first day. What will they think of you?

Activity

Work out how you would cope. Possibilities are:
1. Have a good laugh at yourself.
2. Complain about it to the other apprentices.
3. Tell the storekeeper and foreman it wasn't fair.
4. Blow your top with the foreman.

Which of these ways of behaving seem to fall in with what you feel most people do? In a small group of four discuss the kinds of labels people might attach to you if you behave in certain ways:

| BIGHEAD | BABY | MAMMY'S BOY | A PROPER CHARLIE |

Make a number of such labels, then work out what sort of behaviour invites the label.

In the situations which follow, the comments in brackets beside the suggested response call the tutor's attention to important areas of discussion.

Situation 2

Explanation

The least experienced worker often finds himself or herself in the 'front man' position. He acts as a buffer between the organisation and the public. Pressure from both sides impinge on him. The result can be a ritual performance, anxiety or exasperation.

Situation
You have a job on the forecourt of a garage. A customer comes for his car, saying that he was told to come back at this time. He asks you to get the mechanic to bring it round. When you speak to the mechanic, he is vague, eventually saying, 'Ask him to come back tomorrow.' The customer is annoyed, saying that he needs his car for his work. 'As it is a small job, would you go back to the mechanic and say that I will wait while it is done.' But the mechanic blows up and yells, 'Tell him to fly off!' Well, you know the customer hasn't wings but needs four wheels. You politely tell the customer the mechanic has a number of other overdue urgent jobs. Despite your courtesy, the customer is really angry.

How do you cope?
1 Ask him to go and see the mechanic himself. (*What will this do to your relationship with a workmate?*)
2 Call in the manager and ask him to cope. (*How will he feel about being put on the spot?*)
3 Remove yourself from the customer by going into the office. (*How will he react?*)
4 Make up a story. Say if he comes back later that evening the car will be ready. (*You won't be on duty and someone else will have to cope.*)

Situation 3

Explanation
Young workers find it extremely hard to deal with situations of exploitation involving peers. The inadequate fellow-worker is not as great a problem as the one who refuses to pull his weight, and who has well developed evasive techniques. He is a Machiavellian type who manipulates others for his own ends.

Situation
You work on the loading bay of a large warehouse. Every day one or two heavy lorries come in, which have to be unloaded quickly because the drivers are on 'turn round' bonus. Your workmate is the nephew of the charge-hand. There is something odd about him because, every time these heavy lorries come in, he is at the far end of the warehouse doing something important or he has

disappeared into the lavatory where he stays for twenty-five minutes, coming out just as the work is finishing. The lorry drivers are fed up. A few will help. But they are also taking it out on you. What will you do?

Suggestions for action

1 Complain to the charge-hand. (*Students can look at their feelings about such relationships in the work setting and explore stereotypes about low-level nepotism.*)

2 Complain to the manager of the section. (*An implicit etiquette exists in industry, which is powerful because it is implicit. A breach such as this renders the young person an object of suspicion for the manager as well as the charge-hand, i.e. 'Have I got a troublemaker?'*)

3 Get the lorry drivers to complain themselves. (*How can this be done constructively?*)

4 Have it out with your fellow worker. (*How do you stop a row developing into a punch-up?*)

5 Adopt your workmate's tactics by going to the cloakroom ten seconds before he does, or by ensuring you have a job to do which can't be left. (*This version of the expedient response embodies 'tit for tat' and again will be endorsed blindly by some students.*)

This situation leads into much important work on relationships between peers in work. Within the worker's protective devices, described at the beginning of the section, will be many examples of exploitation of peer by peer. A related situation is:

The maintenance man who never hurries

You are a machine operator who is on a basic rate plus a piecework bonus. In other words, the more you produce the more you get. The maintenance man is lazy, wasting time, chatting up the girls. When your machine breaks down he leaves you for as long as possible. Last time you were idle for nearly an hour. When you went to him and tried to get him to come he sneered, 'We've got a bosses' man here, I can see.' But he did repair the machine, although he still took his time. How would you improve your relationship with him and cope with the situation better?

Students may suggest crude confrontative or aggressive techniques which exacerbate the problem. The strategy will aim at improving relationships so that he does not deliberately procrastinate.

Situation 4

Explanation

I have found that the way and the point at which the first serious mistake occurs is important in work adjustment. Loss of face and feelings of inadequacy can precipitate self-defeating attempts to cover up mistakes. Too high a level of risk is involved at times. Workers then 'take a chance' and react aggressively or blame others when the error is discovered. Judgements of supervisors are often shaped by the worker's reaction to mistakes, therefore positive ways of coping are essential.

> *Situation*
> You are an invoice and general clerk in a large open office. Yesterday at about 15.45 some new type of invoices were placed on your desk. You did them and sent them forward. When you came in this morning, more of them were given to you. As you did the first one, something clicked. You realised you were doing them incorrectly and that you hadn't understood the task. What will you do about those you sent forward yesterday – they may have gone off to the customers?
>
> 1 Would you go and ask for them back, if that is possible?
> 2 Would you immediately go the supervisor and explain to her what has happened?
> 3 Would you take a chance and wait and see? (*This draws attention to the existence of certain attitudes in workers.*)
> 4 If the supervisor has discovered the error and comes to tell you about it, is your reaction that of blaming her for not doing her job properly? (*This makes students look at the attribution of blame, its consequences, and the link with external control which erodes responsibility for one's own actions.*)

The setting is important. This is an open-plan office where visibility is high. Mistakes may be visible, and so will argument. How will supervisors feel when confronted in a public situation? The visibility aspect of mistakes can be taken further.

> You work in a large department store. The rule is: NEVER RUN.
> You realise that a batch of goods in the stock room has been left there. You should have brought them down. Your floor manager has commented on your forgetfulness before, so you decide to dash up in a quiet moment and get them. As you run round the corner you knock into a pile of cartons and the top one falls off with a

sinister sound of breaking glass. A dead silence falls – everybody seems to be looking at you – the floor manager is approaching. How will you cope?

Situation 5

Explanation

Young workers usually detest being the only young person in a group of older workers. The generation conflict is often not initiated by young workers, but they have to cope. The complications can be examined by decision-making exercises of the type given below.

Situation

You have managed to get an apprenticeship. Your first three days were spent following an interesting induction course run by the personnel officers. Many issues were covered, including safety procedures. Now it is over. The training seems to be based on the old principle of 'Do as Nelly does', i.e., you go to an older worker for six weeks and he works alongside you, instructing you, as a supplement to what you learn elsewhere.

When you get to him, he looks at you and says, 'Now, look here! I've been with this firm thirty-five years – man and boy. Don't you take any notice of that lot up in the office – they don't know what they're talking about. Just let me catch you doing them daft safety things and you've had it!'

But you have seen the point and recognised the sense of what you were taught in the induction course. Yet you have to work with him. Do you:

1 Try to put him right? (*Initial interaction shapes judgements, and rigid people will not modify initial impressions.*)
2 Assure him you appreciate he has a lot to teach you and you are ready to learn. Privately you determine to follow safety procedures carefully, guessing that he will not really interfere.
3 Consult the personnel department without making a fuss.
4 Ask your father's advice.
5 Play his game and hope for the best.

There are indications that older workers can be unscrupulous about the safety of young people. This is, by no means, a universal tendency. But if an accident occurs, older workers collude with one another, and the blame is placed on the new entrant. Other aspects of the tensions between managerial instructions and worker adaptations to them should be covered.

Situation 6

Explanation
Loss of face and embarrassment call out defensive and self-defeating responses. False accusations trigger off aggression, which leads to unnecessary trouble. The social-modelling tape on John and the X07 tracksuits described in Chapter 3 can be used, or the following situation:

> *Situation*
> The section leader has come to see your foreman. After discussion they approach you. They ask if you can remember what you did with an expensive instrument you drew from the store ten days ago. They show you the receipt docket you signed when you got it out and the lack of a signature for return. The implication, you feel, is that you did not return it!
> In fact, you did. When your turn came in the queue, the storeman could not find the docket. He said, 'Let me have it, and I'll sort it out in the morning.' You thought no more of it. Now you are faced with this. What do you do?
> 1 State your case, and ask if they will come with you to the store?
> 2 Get angry when stating your case, blaming the storeman?
> 3 Be flippant and not take it seriously, saying you flogged it in the market?

Students should realise that aggressive responses change the nature of the situation from one of enquiry to one of escalating conflict. The unthinking accuser is convinced of the guilt of the worker, although no evidence exists.

Situation 7

Explanation
Young workers are often unaware of the sanctions that can be used by other workers informally against them. The lad who alienates the girl who seams tins on his production belt or the operators can find himself in difficulties. He has breached the behavioural norms, so they respond by breaking the latent agreements about pacing.

> *Situation*
> You have managed to upset the girl who puts the bottoms on the large tins of milk powder which you have to pack. She is now

> retaliating. Every so often, she goes at top speed and jams the belt. Her friends who operate the hoppers are joining her in this. You have to open the carton, staple it, pack it with six tins, and then seal it. Cases have to be put on the truck platform. You just can't cope. When the belt is full, she yells to her friends and makes despairing gestures to the supervisor, who will sometimes help, but who is getting fed up. You feel everybody thinks you are a fool – perhaps you were when you tried to be clever with the girl who is doing all this. How do you cope?
> 1 Ask for your cards?
> 2 Approach the supervisor and explain what all this is about?
> 3 Try to talk to the girl? If this is your answer, how will you approach her?
> 4 Soldier on, hoping things will change for the better?

Discussion should be as free as possible, the tutor entering to make minimal suggestions rather than provide an answer.

Other aspects of adjustment to work
The 'lads' described by Willis (1978) may find any attempt to look at standards and commitment irrelevant. Training for them is only of interest if it leads to jobs with good money. They may deride some of the situations which follow because their basic approach in work of 'Get them before they get you' becomes 'Exploit them before they exploit you.' One problem, not fully faced at times, is whether returning to school or entering college is an appropriate action for those who have rejected education or have felt themselves to be rejected by it. We should, however, pay some attention to it even if some students are disinterested.

Situation 8

Explanation
Jobs are being taken by those who would not have considered them a few years ago. Ambitious young workers often do not know how to express keenness without attracting resentment and ridicule.

> *Situation*
> You have gone into a factory because there seemed to be no other opportunity open to you in the area where you live. You are determined to make a success of it and carve out a career in the firm. The supervisors approve of you, and all was well until a fortnight ago. Since then you have been getting an increasing

number of nasty comments, and the names 'boot-licker' and 'foreman's bootboy' are directed at you. Tension seems to be growing, and you feel you must cope with this development. Would you:
1 Decide you must weather the storm?
2 Discuss it with the supervisors?
3 Have it out with the worst offender?
4 Let fellow workers know it is upsetting you?
5 Some other action. (*If so, what would it be?*)

There is no set recipe for action. Students must be encouraged to identify the conditions in which certain responses are likely to work.

A whole unit of guidance for adjustment to work could centre on:
1 The need to attain credibility and acceptance in a working group before criticising and making suggestions for change. Students have to learn they must make limited task-related statements in their early encounters in working groups. Many young workers do not understand why they receive adverse responses from others and fail to see their own contribution to this situation.
2 Processes in working groups which trap new workers into making unfortunate statements about supervision, working conditions and the product, which are then retailed with gusto and exaggeration.
3 Presentation of self. Students should examine the signals they send to others. Can they put their viewpoint firmly without brashness or arrogance? By unwillingness to join in things and to offer a hand when necessary, the young worker conveys an unattractive picture of himself.

Situation 9

Explanation
'It's not my job,' is a statement heard within a strict division of labour. It acts as a justification for ignoring difficulties. Yet, if at school and college we invest energy in instilling standards of excellence, it would only be sensible to anticipate challenges to those standards.

Situation
You work in a small factory. You are responsible for the last operation on the refrigerators made by the firm – placing a label on

top. You are interested in electrical work, however, and note that the earth wiring seems to be defective. The machines have been inspected. All that will happen is that during the evening a part-time shift will pack the refrigerators and send them for despatch. It's two minutes to five – you finish at five. It's not your job, but what do you think you should do about it?

I have found it better to use this situation to open up a general discussion.

Situation 10

Explanation

We need to identify tension points and inoculate students against them. We may teach telephone skills, but do we teach students to use them under conditions of noise and distraction?

Situation

A simple open office situation is arranged. Students work in groups of six. They discuss how they will undertake the simulation before they begin. One will add up, but be interrupted by a query; another will be given instructions while answering the telephone.

A discussion about coping should follow.

The skills of a job search

Much excellent work has been published in this area. No attempt will be made to duplicate this. The section will highlight facets of the topic which are given insufficient attention. Research, e.g., Sawdon *et al* (1981) suggests that young people eventually get a job if they persist. But the period of unemployment is lengthening, and it can be two years before they find work. Maintenance of positive attitudes is difficult. Coupled with the need to seize opportunities vigorously, this makes the skills of a job search a salient part of 16 - 19 guidance. Experience shows key aspects to be:

Key areas of a job search

1 Finding out about the firm and its products.
2 Filling in application forms accurately and neatly.
3 Writing competent letters of application.
4 Telephone skills.

> 5 Responding to the cues sent by the interviewer.
> 6 Asking questions which convey a good impression of the applicant.

Interviewers are put off when they discover the applicant claiming keenness has little knowledge of the firm or the job for which he has applied. A few enquiries would remedy this. Even the sympathetic interview is irritated when the young person seems blind to the implication of his questions and stolidly refuses to respond to the cues that he receives. Questions asked by candidates can reflect a negative image of which they are blissfully unaware. Clearly, many applicants have never been taught to think about the impression conveyed by their queries. Questions about holidays and pay are legitimate, but if the applicant has already been informed about them in writing, the interviewer properly wonders about the ability or motivation of the interviewee. Students can be taught to ask questions which communicate enthusiasm and interest, as part of efficient self-preservation.

The following guidance activities have provided a foundation for prolonged searches for work:

1 *Survey the scene with friends*
With a small group of friends make an informal agreement to help each other in searching for a job.

Select a number of firms you would like to investigate.

Ask critical questions.
- Is this firm one which seems to be expanding or is it likely to lay off people?
- If it merits further investigation, what sorts of jobs may be available? Unskilled work may be obtainable when apprenticeships are not.
- Do we have friends or relatives who can alert us to the possibility of a job in the offing?
- What does each firm make? Is it a complete product or do they make components for other firms? You may need to ask questions about stability of demand, if the latter is the case.

Make a start on the survey
Look for advertisements and scan the cards at the Job Centre to get a better idea of available jobs.

List the questions you want answered. The group should decide how their findings will be recorded, so that the information can be shared.

Tutors should direct investigation to the stereotypes of certain firms or jobs. Some production processes entail an enduring smell which attaches itself to the worker, allowing identification on a bus, etc. A reputation – usually of doubtful validity – is sometimes allocated to workers in certain firms. Exploration is vital because young people rarely question such stereotypes.

2 *What does the interviewer want?*
A first step is for the small group to discuss what they think the interviewer expects when he says:

'Would you be prepared to - - -?'
'What do you think you might find difficult?'
'Do you get on well with older people?'
'How long do you think you might stay if we did offer you the job?'
'What do you do in your spare time?'
'Can you work in a group of women/men?'
'What do you have to give the job?'
'Tell me how you think other people might describe you?'

After discussion of a particular response, an interviewer is heard on tape commenting on what he hopes to find out by asking the question.

Question: 'What do you think you might find difficult?'
Interviewer: 'I ask this because it helps me learn whether the applicant has found out something about the job. If he hasn't, he soon flounders. You also get an idea of how honest he is – if he flannels, it's obvious. I know applicants are anxious and want a job, but although I'm sympathetic, I don't like it when they try to put one across me. "What are they going to be like in work?" is what I then ask myself. It's always best to be honest.

'If they reply, "Nothing", then I'm worried. It means they haven't thought about noise, heat and other demands of the factory floor. If they don't know, but admit it, and try to look at possibilities, then I'm impressed.'

Question: 'What do you think other people would say about you?'
Interview: 'In this job people have to work together. If somebody can't get on with the others, productivity falls. Also, some of our young workers have a lot to do with the public, and tense situations develop when orders are not ready as promised. If somebody is big-headed, over-anxious or rude, it makes things worse. If they show me that they know their weak spots and can be honest, I'm reassured. I usually go on, and ask more directly about how they control themselves when somebody is aggressive or irritating.'

Students can construct their own lists of questions that have been asked in interviews, examining the reasons why they are asked and the best way of replying.

3 Students could examine a series of short responses.
Customer: 'What did you say?'
Salesgirl: 'Nothing. Why?'
Customer: 'I'm sorry, I thought you were saying thank you.'

4 Students often fail to understand the importance of dress at work. Tensions emanate from failure to adapt to demands – young people appear to think that rules are flexible and can be disregarded with impunity. In general career guidance I begin by discussing preferences about the type of clothes which will be worn at work. The concepts and issues of uniform are explored. Uniform can be seen as a way of temporarily suspending other identities, bringing the work role to the forefront. Servicemen, nurses, police and other uniformed workers make statements about themselves through their uniform. Young people may welcome this emphasis on vocational self or find it an intolerable restriction. Body image is often dismissed in 16 - 19 guidance, yet, in conjunction with the presentation of self through dress, it preoccupies young people. The strong vocational identity provided by uniform is paralleled by the limits to dress in other occupations. Inter-generational conflict at work is sometimes triggered off by breaches of dress rules. Discussion of these issues, which are often ignored, is a useful form of anticipation. Simple exercises which push students towards taking the standpoint of others are advocted. An approach for the more academic follows.

Situation
You are nineteen, fashion conscious in a rather extreme way, and somewhat critical of the middle-aged. The firm you have joined as a junior secretary is a traditional one, full of rather dowdy creatures. The senior secretary has made occasional disapproving comments, e.g. 'It seems that girls today have no colour or dress sense.' Yesterday, she approached you formally, requesting you to come to work today in appropriate clothing. (She did not define 'appropriate'.) Your response was to wear your most outlandish outfit as a challenge. She comes to you, asking if you would be kind enough to come to her office to discuss the matter.

1 Now write the interview as if it were a script for television.
2 Write what you both said and did on the left-hand half of the paper.
3 But, as soon as you have done this, go to the right-hand half and write down the unspoken things that you imagine to be in the mind of the speaker. Your first two entries might look like this (remember you are the young junior secretary).

What the senior secretary or I said or did	What was in her mind or my mind as we spoke or acted
1 Senior Secretary Jean, I am sorry to have to speak to you again about dress, but the firm's rules are strict.	I hate doing this but if I don't she'll be dismissed. Why can't she co-operate?
2 Junior Secretary It seems petty. I do my work well. Does it matter?	I've got to stand up for myself, but how can I keep my end up?

4 Allow 20 minutes. Always go from left to right as shown above.
5 Make notes on the discrepancies between what was said and what was in the minds of the speakers.
What beliefs were held? What were the important points in the interaction which seemed to determine what happened?
6 Discuss and compare your scripts in small groups of three.

5 Application forms

Most firms have social consciences and will help with guidance activities if approached, providing that requests are reasonable. They usually give permission for duplication of application forms. The use of duplicated forms gives a greater realism to the activity below.

Step 1
Small group discussion (7 - 10 minutes) on:
- Handwriting. Is it a good idea to fill in every section in capital letters, unless requested?
- Accuracy of birth year. Why is it important?
- How to cope if O-level or CSE results are requested, but the examinations have not yet been taken.
- The advantages and snags of filling in the form using pencil first.
- The best way of correcting errors.

Step 2
Partner work on feelings about filling in forms. The errors the student feels he habitually makes can also be discussed (7 - 10 minutes).

Step 3
The first form to be used for practice is filled in. Partners check one another's form. Discussion follows.

Follow-up activities
Practice with a number of different forms is essential. One productive variation is to duplicate a form containing a number of errors made by the candidate – spelling, illegibility and errors of fact. Students are then given a blank replica and asked to fill it in, correcting the errors in the first form. Benefit comes from a brief discussion of the usual fate of incomplete and inaccurate forms when processed by hard-pressed clerks.

6 *Letters of application*
The full horror of the inadequacies of letters of application is seen when one inspects a large sample of letters received by a firm. Attention must be paid to:
   – The negative impact of letters written on lined paper, often obviously from exercise books.
   – The need to check details before posting. In one batch I noted two letters without addresses. Doubtless two people were complaining that the firm did not bother to acknowledge applications.
   – Assessment of the reaction of readers to spelling errors.

Tutor work could begin by students considering the impact on the recipient of this letter of application for the post of junior secretary:

26, Chapelhay Rd,
Newtown
Widnes W1X 02E

Dear Sir,
I am writing to apply for the post of junior secretary for which I am well suited. I have spent a year studying typing and shorthand. Could you send me full details of renummeration and hours.
Also hollidays.
I await for your reply which I hope willcome as soon as possible.
Yours truly
Jane Smith

Tutors can use the excellent material published on this topic. But application-writing is a skill, and should be practised regularly.

7 Telephone skills

Young people searching for work suffer erosion of confidence which manifests itself when they have to initiate action. Incompetence on the telephone can be costly. Clerks and telephonists have little conscience about the bungling caller when lines are busy – especially when arrogance or petulance have irritated them. Simple points merit consideration, e.g.

1. Have plenty of change when calling from a public box. Even if the call is a short one, boxes often reject coins. Confused caller and irritated recipient do not make a good start.
2. Explain briefly what the call is about. If applicants have been requested to ask for Ms J. Able, do that. If no details are given, ask to be connected with someone dealing with the advertised job. Ask politely for an appointment, writing it down, and repeating time, date and other details as a check. Get the name of the person to whom you are speaking and their extension number. Do not forget to say thank you.
3. Comparison of different approaches when making enquiries is enlightening. Males mask their uncertainty by 'chatting up', which gets short shrift.

Role play is helpful, although it is better done after listening to a taped excerpt such as this:

Caller   It's about the job – the one advertised tonight in the paper. Can I speak to the manager?

Telephonist   It will be better if I put you through to Mrs Green. She handles all job enquiries.

Caller   Yes, I suppose so, but I'd really like to speak to the manager.

Telephonist   Just let me put you through – the switchboard is very busy.

Mrs Green   Personnel, Mrs Green. Can I help you?

Caller   Yes, I'm interested in the job in tonight's *Echo*.

Mrs Green   Could you please tell me which one you are after. We advertised three tonight.

Caller   Oh, I didn't notice. It's the one for a junior clerk to do general office duties and filing. I've done a lot of that at school, and my mother liked working in an office. Mrs Jones, our careers mistress, said office work was interesting, so I thought I might just as well have a go. My sister's a writer in the Wrens.

Mrs Green   Well, it sounds as if you have some interest, even if you didn't read the advertisement carefully. We asked applicants to send for our usual application form, enclosing a stamped, addressed envelope. Could you do that, please? By the way, what is your full name and address? I'd better make a note of it.

Students discuss the significance of Mrs Green's final point. Anxiety often makes people fail to register salient points, and introduce incoherency and irrelevancy as this girl did.

Mutual support in searching for a job

Group discussion is most productive in exploring this area. Tutors should help pupils anticipate stress. There can be no evasions. Yet we must be positive. The first step is for friends to form groups to offer mutual support and share information. They should be taught how to make links with firms, getting to know foremen and other useful people. I have a tape-recording of an eighteen year-old worker who was out of work for almost two years. His advice to people seeking a job was that they should use the Jobcentre and Careers Service, but not rely on them alone. This advice has been sound in many cases. Groups of friends seeking work should enrol relatives and other people as sources of information. Young people are often unaware of resources available. The Thompson Report (1982) accepts that youth work is concerned with social education. It is also a major source of guidance and support for the unemployed. Tutors must make this clear to students and develop links with the Youth Service, which has been undervalued.

Life style is a fundamental concept in careers guidance. It is equally important in the mainenance of self-respect during a period of unemployment. Delinquency is largely opportunist rather than planned. The unemployed have a life style marked by passivity and minimal satisfactions. Fatalistic acceptance of unemployment as something which happens and has to be put with, implies that the unemployed are powerless. Tutors have to gather courage and examine this.

Scrounging and borrowing are predominant features of the life style of unemployed young people. They borrow from friends and attempt to repay them. Parents are not often repaid. Tensions centre on money and passivity. The parent who comes in exhausted to find son and daughter with feet up and a pile of unwashed coffee cups is likely to explode. Behind apparent indifference to the feelings of parents is erosion of self-respect. Patterns of staying up later and rising later seem to be associated with fatalism. Unless a sense of potency has been maintained, negative predictions increase when the possibility of a job appears: the young person predicts failure and does not try to get it.

If this is reality and we have compassion as educators, then we must look at these issues. Students must express anxieties and doubts in a supportive climate. This means honesty and realism. False hopes must not be boosted, but neither can fatalism be encouraged.

Guidance and unemployment

Endorsement of the importance of family involvement and of the use of local contacts is found in the Lewisham Study (Edwards and Morris, 1981). Easter leavers seemed to be particularly successful in getting a job by such means. Those responsible for 16 - 19 guidance must, however, face unpalatable facts. A limited opportunity structure cannot be changed by guidance. We simply help students compete more efficiently. Young people may have realistic job aspirations, but this is no guarantee that they fit the job market.

The signposts to the future are difficult to read, if not obliterated. Dramatic predictions have to be treated cautiously, as Taylor (1981) points out, but it seems likely that long-term structural unemployment stemming from technological innovations will increase. Traditional curricula and sources of motivation become irrelevant as the school loses its credentialist position. Graduate unemployment is already common. Problems of order and control – always salient in teaching – may absorb teacher energy. Fortunately, we have time to work out our strategies and response as there will be a transitional period due to cultural and technological lag.

Currently, we have little knowledge of the effects of unemployment. Evidence drawn from the 'thirties' is suspect because expectations, social context and beliefs are now different. Some writers find no evidence of erosion of the work ethic. Others, e.g., Seabrook (*Guardian* 22.11.1982), see the generation gap manifested in the fact that work identity has been crucial for the middle-aged, but is of little concern to the young. Is work a necessary part of identity? Those offering guidance must see that they have been conditioned to see occupational identity as prime. We would all escape these frightening issues if we could. Denial or blind blame is of no help.

The stigma of unemployment and devaluation of the unemployed obscure the fact that people can maintain integrity and act constructively during a period of unemployment. This does not deny the pain, humiliation or the need to recast our social measures. The stress may come from social and psychological forces, including poverty, and not from lack of traditional employment. We tend to blame the unemployed, or to look for those who are to blame and who should 'do something about it'. Emotive judgements focus on the few who avoid work or manipulate the situation. Open minds and avoidance of early closure are essential. As Campbell (1981) argues, the rejection of work may be a protective mechanism when the individual has met successive rejections and disappointments. Equally, we cannot assume that certain stresses or forms of disturbance are a direct consequence of unemployment. They could be antecedent conditions which contributed to unemployment.

Females seem to suffer more than males. Edwards and Morris (1981) mention parental reinforcement of the girl as a temporary worker. I have noted that they tend to become isolated within the home, especially when their mother works or when they live in rural districts. Males are tending to move in greater numbers into jobs where females were previously in the majority. Nursing, hairdressing, catering and certain types of retail trade provide examples. There seem no signs of a substantial counter-move by females. Kramer (1982) reports that girls experience different and more severe social difficulties than boys when unemployed. Social isolation is enhanced because friends who work are reluctant to share new experiences, out of concern for the girl's feelings. Awkwardness is resolved by creating social distance. Boys have problems centred on money. Subsidisation by friends when drinking, for example, makes for unease. For boys, however the experience of unemployment is more likely to be a group one, and so less sharp in its impact. As Kramer's respondents describe it, the situation is one of 'All borrowing from one another, and nobody can pay it back.'

The basic issues
It is vital to search for ways of compensating for the loss of the exchange relationship, in order to preserve the self-respect and social integration of those without traditional employment. This is a profound social question and cannot be the responsibility of the school. We can, however, look at the issue, encouraging students to preserve self-respect through meaningful voluntary exchange relationships. This will not be acceptable to all students, or within the capacity of some. Guidance has to encourage young people to develop a structure for living and an anchorage in the community which are personally significant.

Discussion and negotiation are crucial. We do not know the answers: even if we did, we have no right to impose them. In 1974 I described counselling as a process of status-equal transactions. In this, the most difficult area of guidance, we must never lose sight of this principle. Tutor and students could discuss the building of a unit of guidance covering:

> **Topics for negotiation in guidance for unemployment**
> 1 Meaningful voluntary extension of community work.
> 2 The skills of building your own job.
> 3 The use of leisure time.
> 4 Coping with stress.
> 5 Understanding family relationships.

If we take community work as a starting point, tutor and students might find themselves considering:

1 Inviting representatives of voluntary agencies which work with the handicapped and other groups to discuss the ways in which someone who is unemployed could contribute. Reports from local youth workers show that their unemployed members often react well to such activities. The insistence upon high standards is welcomed by the volunteers.
2 The enlistment of local radio in the search for new forms of exchange relationship. This is also a potent source for counter-acting negative stereotypes about young unemployed where it matters – in the neighbourhood.
3 The building of links between school or college and the youth service. What is begun in the formal education service should be carried on, and further developed in the informal setting.
4 The development of counselling skills in students. They trust one another and try to help, but often would like to know more about ways of doing it.
5 It has been found helpful in some youth clubs to use the 'unemployment coach', i.e., a young person who, whilst actively striving to find work, is also leading a satisfying life. For students such a person can be a credible source of information to whom they confide anxieties without fearing negative assessment. (Parents and others will have to be consulted. Local newspapers can still produce headlines, such as, *Teaching them to enjoy life on the dole*.)

This realism may appear intimidating. But young people respect honesty and despise evasion. They see teachers as not knowing much about life and having little to say that is relevant. Students have to face the fact that after enthusiastic involvement in a course of training they may find themselves without work, and tutors should not hide it. Good guidance anticipates, and helps provide ways of coping, taking into account that it can be more difficult for girls than for boys, particularly as provision of leisure activities for girls is poorer.

Ideas for inclusion in a module

1 *Exploring possibilities*
A small group – two to four students – explores ways of contacting and visiting representatives of local organisations to ask relevant questions.
– How can young people contribute in a responsible way?
– What attitudes and skills will the volunteers need?*
– What training and support will be available?
– What are the challenges?

If representatives come to the school, this group should be responsible for the organisation and act as hosts.

2 *Counselling skills*
Helping relationships are fostered when students have access to the skills of counselling. Attention can be paid to:
1 The skills of active listening, i.e., letting the problem emerge.
2 The need to avoid giving superficial advice or persuasion. Peers often believe they should find a solution or recommend a course of action.
3 The advisability of taking the 'one step at a time' approach.

Tutors can help students use apparently naïve approaches productively. Stress can be pictured as a person carrying a bucket of water which is full to the brim and slopping over. What can be done to prevent spillage? Students learn that they can help peers to function adequately by relieving minor areas of stress, even if they cannot change the main situation. This 'threshold theory' asks the practical question, 'What can be done to make life tolerable?' Much of Chapters 2 and 3 can be helpful to students. Certainly, understanding of predictions and the forces which shape behaviour is welcomed by them. Friends spend a great deal of time discussing shared problems, but feel they need more knowledge. The principle is that of Alcoholics Anonymous and similar organisations: helping

---

* Discussion of relationships is necessary, especially if the helped are in the same age group as the helpers. Girls respond to the handicapped boy – perhaps too intensely – but boys may be insensitive to the emotional needs of the handicapped girl. Danger of exploitation exists on both sides, no less dangerous because it is unintentional.

reinforces a positive self-image. Tutors can use this approach as a teaching method which enables students to develop their own coping strategies.

Practice can be given by simple situations, examples of which are given below.

Situation 1
Four of your friends have been unemployed for over a year. Tensions have developed at home, so the two boys and two girls decide it might be a good idea to move into a flat. They are just good friends who knock around together. The girls and one of the boys go steady with other people. They mention the situation to you and ask what you think. Is it a good idea? Look at this situation very practically.

(Escape from difficulties is often attempted by this ploy. The result is often disastrous.)

Situation 2
You have a good friend who is 19 years old. He is very worried about something when you meet him. You know he has worried about his failure to get a job. As you drink a lager with him he tells you he is in real trouble. He fancies himself as a musician, although he isn't much good, in fact, and went out when he was fed up and bought a lot of equipment. He gave some false information on the hire purchase form. The store didn't check even although it was a *No deposit* offer. Now he can't pay the current instalment. He knows he won't be able to pay the future ones. He asks, 'What do you think I should do?' How would you try to help him? Think very carefully about it.

(Unemployed young people feel deprived. They sometimes express their frustration through impulsive and irrational spending sprees. They know it doesn't solve any problems, but they still cannot stop themselves. Anticipation will not always prevent them behaving in this way, but they can look at ways of coping when they have done it.)

Situation 3
The youth club in your district takes people up to the age of twenty. You normally attend regularly, but illness has kept you away for a month. Several of the older ones have a reputation for being tough and have been involved in crime. You have two friends who attend the club. When you meet them they tell you they've 'bought it'. They went on a breaking and entering job with two of the toughs. One of your friends had borrowed his father's

car to transport the stolen goods. He was stopped by the police, who identified the goods. Now they are both in a sweat. Their panic was increased because of the threats of the older blokes: 'Shop us, and - - -'. What do you help them think about? What action should they take?

(Tutors can follow this up if they wish. Crime is sometimes associated with unemployment, especially the adolescent offences of vandalism, breaking and entering, taking away and driving cars without consent. We must not communicate the belief that the unemployed will commit crimes, for many do not. They may express sympathy with those who commit offences, but this does not mean they will take up active roles as delinquents. They may want to know how to resist the invitation to get involved without losing face.)

3 *Using leisure time*

Fleming and Lavercombe (1982) point out that for many young people having so much time on your hands is the worst feature of unemployment. The unemployment coach can make suggestions, but more structured help is needed. Tutors could examine with students:

1 The leisure facilities available at low cost in the neighbourhood.
2 The construction of a personal inventory of interests and abilities available for leisure activities.
3 Reactions to physical challenge and social demands. Many males react to physical challenge and risk positively, e.g., parachuting and diving. Others find they like leadership roles in social situations where the limelight is turned on them. Awareness of such tendencies helps them match leisure activities to preferences.
4 The tutorial groups should get to know youth club personnel. Wardens welcome members who will take responsibility and participate in club management. Recognition of the 'on-demand' counselling provided by the youth service provides a bulwark against apathy and resignation, which is the great problem of the unemployed.

Exchange relationships

Generic vocational skills have to be relevant to what is happening, or going to happen, in the lives of young adults. We have to ask if the vocational skills are for jobs that will be available in the future, or for jobs that are currently available but are declining. Sometimes people stress the importance for the unemployed of the informal economy, which has always been present in industrial society, but as Caplovitz (1974) shows, it is used by those who have acquired marketable skills and who are in work. Loose reference to it as a source of income for the young unemployed reflects undue optimism.

The exchange relationship with society has to be revised. This demands political action. Answers will emerge gradually as part of painful social change in which our basic perceptions of traditional employment will have to be recast. The creation of a new frame of reference is beyond guidance. In the transitional period we can teach pupils the skills of exploiting such opportunities as exist, of making their own job and marketing. Entrepreneurial skills can be stimulated. Initiative training does not have to be restricted to the physical, it can be economically based. The word 'entrepreneurial' implies considered risk-taking. The objective is to give young adults a chance to consider exchange relationships outside the traditional worker role. Self-sufficiency has been debated in many ways in recent years and should be part of guidance.

Before going further, I must stress the complications. I have no clear answers, only tentative strategies which need to be evaluated, sharpened or discarded as the situation changes. Hypocrisy exists, and is an ever-present trap. The attitude of blaming the unemployed, subjecting them to judgements which imply they have chosen to be unemployed, is accompanied by condemnation if they show initiative and make a little money. One young man remarked, 'I'm damned if I do, and I'm damned if I don't.' The position is both complex and punitive.

Young people can be reduced to impotency by legalisms, yet the fact that they can do something and make some extra money for themselves is crucial to keeping self-respect alive. Ideas such as Young Enterprise have shown what can be achieved. Chemistry departments in schools have made cosmetics and ginger beer, whilst the contribution of the crafts and design departments is obvious. Cleaning, gardening, traditional crafts, making plastics and other activities of self-help may have to be developed. None of this implies collusion in the creation of shoddy jobs (which is how young people and their parents often see work experience). It means that we consider job creation a legitimate activity for young people. We move from a negative concept of survival skills to a positive one of exploiting opportunities and making an impact on what can still be a malleable world.

> A guidance project might consist of:
> 1 A survey by the tutor group of potential markets for particular services in the locality.
> 2 Assessment of potential snags, i.e., people cannot get gardeners, but the need is seasonal, therefore it has to be integrated with other non-seasonal activities.
> 3 Exploring the economics, e.g., the equipment necessary.
> 4 Planning, publicity and accounting.
> 5 Providing a reliable service.

Anticipating stress and changed family relationships in unemployment
Depression, whether overt or masked, is the factor which has to be dealt with in unemployment. The first vacation passes as previous ones; the search for a job continues optimistically; self-doubt emerges occasionally, but is stifled; eventually, misgivings crystallise into the realisation that unemployment will be long-term, if not permanent, and depression sets in. Understanding of the process aids self-control, allowing the individual to insulate himself against the self-erosion.

Guidance should anticipate and reduce vulnerability to self-destructive blame by giving students the opportunity to discuss the social and technological causes of unemployment. Those from homes where the emphasis is on 'what the neighbours will think' have sometimes internalised these values and see unemployment as a personal condemnation. Feelings of being cheated should be explored honestly. Disrupted expectations and the long-term sense of a career which has been challenged by the prospect of unemployment are issues not to be evaded. Learning what the processes are prevents the growth of helplessness and passivity.

Depression
In guidance for the 16 - 19 year group we are concerned with reactive depression which originates in the life space and the consequent problems of the individual. Depression is marked by weaker interaction with the environment, a sense of worthlessness and helplessness. Rowe (1978) states that modern therapies stress:
1 The element of self-reproach.
2 The fact that depression is worst early in the morning. (I have found this important when helping depressed and out-of-work young people.)
3 Low expectations of change in the depressed person.

Rutter (1975) shows that depression in the adolescent is associated with loss of appetite, sleeplessness, irritability, loss of concentration and physical complaints such as headaches or gastro-intestinal difficulties. Unemployed young people demonstrate these symptoms at times. It has been helpful to discuss with them the way in which other fears are translated into worries about health. Fears about health and physical survival often occur in this age group, although they hide them from those they see as unsympathetic. Parental anxieties often reinforce the depression of the unemployed. The well-meaning parent who urges the depressed young person to go out, do something interesting, or bring friends in is sometimes unwittingly making him feel more helpless. Bringing these situations into the open encourages better coping. Depression makes people build a wall around themselves. They separate themselves from others, simultaneously wanting to change, and yet preventing it. Guidance sessions put students into control. An introductory approach I have used is:

1 List the ways someone could react to continued failure to get a job.
2 Discuss your list with a friend. Look for hidden reactions – like pretending not to mind.
3 Now imagine you have left school/college and find you cannot get a job. How will you feel?
4 Work out with a group of friends the ways in which you could cope.
5 Tutor and group discussion follows.

Later sessions would look at parental reactions to depression, and students' likely responses. Students are taught that the first rule for positive survival is to understand what is happening. It is essential to discuss carefully – using the principles of Chapters 2 and 3 – the ways in which depression can be marked by arrogance, by assuming the role of the life and soul of the party or by indulging in superficially daring behaviours such as speeding. The approach should be factual. A cognitive approach is required which, whilst recognising feelings, stresses ways of coping. This will not eradicate the problem, but it seems to help control and limit reactions. Unemployment may precipitate difficulties which would have been contained by the structure to daily life provided by employment.

Awareness of the impact of unemployment on family relationships is needed, but often is not provided. The family provides its members with identities, building into the individual dominant values and expectations which form the bedrock for self-evaluation. It filters out, sharpens or amplifies uniquely some of those forces we call social class. Above all, it creates a symbolic environment through which the outside world and transactions with it assume meaning. Some families strengthen a sense of the world as threatening, others stress respectability and the evaluations of authority figures. Where the family background is that of the respectable artisan, loss of or failure to get a job is interpreted in the moral terms of the Protestant ethic. This creates, at the extremes, vulnerability to depression or a defensive rejection of the need to work.

Students need to understand how family attitudes affect their ability to cope with unemployment. As yet we know very little, but we can ask meaningful questions. If a sense of helplessness and passivity is induced by the home, how does this shape the young adult's reaction to unemployment? If work is seen as necessary for self-respect, as evidence of virtue and as a pre-condition for acceptability, how does this influence adjustment to long-term unemployment? How does susceptibility to the evaluations of others and an ethic which stresses shame, influence the young adult? Group and individual counselling in which I have been involved provided evidence that the more intelligent young person is concerned with these issues.

The unemployed father is often a problem for his children. Even during a strike I met pupils reacting sharply to their fathers' expression of frustration. The father's role is still seen as primarily anchored in the world of work. When unemployed, he may feel unwanted at home and an impediment. He can seek compensation for his loss of authority and power by turning the home into an arena. The unemployed son or daughter becomes the focus for blame and criticism. Students must understand that the unemployed father can project his self-dislike or anxieties on to his children. He watches their movements closely, questioning them in a provocative way. Outline of such scenes can be taped. Attention-seeking behaviour is common. Food is the focus for complex emotions in the family, e.g., anorexia nervosa. I have found that many tensions centre on mealtimes and food in the homes of the unemployed. Kramer (1982) found that young unemployed he interviewed experienced denial of food or over-eating in their unemployed fathers. Disturbed marital relationships, and drinking or aggression used as devices to reduce tension are common. Young people have asked me for help with coping with the father's coercive control, irrationality and unpredictability. They need to be helped to maintain their self-control, avoid counter-provocation without feeling humiliated or weak, offer a measure of understanding and, crucially, use the experience for self-development.

> *An example of a tape*
> Father and daughter are involved. A commentator makes remarks to help underline the points.
>
> | | |
> |---|---|
> | *Father* (as daughter comes into the house) | I wonder where she's been? It's about time I checked up. You don't know what's going on these days. |
> | *Daughter* (coming into room) | Hi, Dad. Anything good on telly tonight? |
> | *Father* (sharply) | Now, my girl, where have you been? It's nearly eleven. |
> | *Commentator* | The inevitable reply follows. |
> | *Daughter* | Out! |
> | *Father* | Now – who have you been with? |
> | *Commentator* | Now wait for the equally inevitable reply. |
> | *Daughter* | Friends! |
> | *Father* | Which friends? |
> | *Commentator* | An almost equally inevitable reply. |
> | *Daughter* | You won't know them. |
> | *Father* | Look here, my girl. You'll be in tomorrow at ten. No later – understand? |
> | *Daughter* (muttering to herself) | If he thinks I'm like that, then I will be. |
> | *Father* | What's that? |
> | *Daughter* (wearily) | Nothing. |
>
> The tutor asks the group to discuss:
> 1. the meaning of the girl's penultimate remark;
> 2. the fact that the father thinks he is concerned, but the girl sees him as distrustful;
> 3. how the girl could handle the situation more constructively.

Parents become anxious, exerting pressure on their son or daughter to achieve, invoking the comparisons mentioned in Chapter 2. Resentment is created. Discussion of the situation below alerts students to ways of coping:

> **Why can't they stop?**
> You did reasonably well in your 5th year, getting reasonable O-levels in maths and English – a B and C respectively. You got

> CSEs in biology and history. No job came your way so you come back into the sixth form to improve your results. Parents are the difficulty – they remind you of the current job situation, of which you are acutely aware. At least once a day you are compared with your brother, who is a sub-manager in a large engineering firm. His progress at Polytechnic, his good degree and other achievements are paraded before you. Your feeling is, 'I'm worried already.' When they go at me like this, I just want to give up.'
>
> Tutor group members discuss:
> 1 How could he reduce the tensions?
> 2 What is the best way of helping the parents understand?

Other aspects of family stress are:
1 Concern expressed negatively because parents fail to see the economic and social causes of unemployment. They try to coerce the young person to try harder.
2 The mother moving into a collusive position with the boy, especially if she works. She provides him with extra money without the father's knowledge.
3 Parents tending to keep their children in an infantile, dependent position, eroding the growth of self-management and responsibility.
4 Parents blaming friends for their child's unemployment. Irrational blame of boy or girl friend frequently occurs. Students can be taught how to avoid provocation and dramatic threats of leaving home.

Guidance must anticipate the impact of sexual stereotypes. They make it difficult for both males and females to accept role change, i.e., that the female may go out to work and the male stay at home. These stereotypes are more than a product of the belief that both marital partners must work to ensure a decent standard of living. Boys find it hard to contemplate the possibility of being dependent upon a female. Interestingly, Kramer (1982) found support for the fact that women still sustain men in a position of dominance in the family.

Unemployment has an impact on sexual relationships. Young people may live together in search of a compensatory warmth in a bleak world, but then they experience financial insecurity and periodic crises of mistrust. Sexual relationships during unemployment seem casual, usually because the partners both feel devalued.

Anxieties rise sharply in parents when a couple become engaged or begin living together. Parents exert strong pressures on the woman.

The mother's anxieties are especially high and difficult to meet because they incorporate strong maternal appeals. Discussion of this is essential – the students probably know more about the possibilities than the tutor. But the tutor can show a proper reticence and let them explore in an accepting climate.

As yet we have little knowledge of how to prepare young people for marriage or its equivalent in a world where neither prospective parent has worked, or is likely to. Whether or not insecurities will have an effect on the child beyond those usually associated with poverty remains uncertain. We do not know how the continuous presence of the father will affect the child-mother relationship. These things lie in the future, yet we need to introduce these topics. We have to admit doubt and ambiguity when we would like to be able to provide clear answers.

We must consider aspects of larger social change, such as divisiveness. New forms of this may be a by-product of technological change. We have seen that loss of exchange relationships may weaken social integration. But a divisive society could also emerge in other ways. An élite group may hold jobs functionally necessary for the creation of wealth and the maintenance of essential services. There may be a second group who hold jobs created as a palliative or as a means of social control, which may carry connotations of artificiality and inferiority. Third, there may be a group who do not have a job, and who are unlikely to obtain one. This group will include graduates, A-level candidates and those who would have taken traditional apprenticeships, for whom work was an essential part of identity. Unemployment is not the preserve of the dull, deviant, disadvantaged, disturbed or delinquent – a fact we often forget.

Next we must look at the pattern of expectations fostered by background and upbringing and the disruption of those expectations. Preferences in gratification have been linked with social class. The working class was alleged to demand immediate gratification, whilst the middle class could defer it by long-term planning and expectations of rational step-by-step advancement. Although the modern world questions this step-by-step progression, socialisation patterns have a compelling hold. The disruption of internalised expectations can be painful and confusing.

If guidance does not face such issues, it could by default be a tool for conditioning people into quiescence. Only later would they discover they had been denied the attitudes and skills allowing them to cope responsibly with a changing society. Negotiation with students is essential – but the tutor has to look at himself critically.

We can only do what we understand, but we can still question why we understand so little.

Careers education

Economic changes have rendered many key concepts of careers education pointless. Stronger doubts about its utility are voiced as unemployment grows. Realistic careers education is actually more important now than in previous years, provided that it embodies the three basic concepts of
1 Field
2 Level
3 Life style.

Careers officers have known that those who made a mistake in the choice of their first job often made the same mistake in choosing the second. No learning occurred. It is doubtful even today that any job is better than no job, and it may be disastrous for a young person to take a job in which he feels ill at east or incompetent.

Field is the broad area of work towards which a person is drawn, e.g., the computational, mechanical, scientific, practical, medical, literary, aesthetic, outdoor or social service. Personality factors of interest, temperament and motivation are prime, but such fields involve aptitudes and skills. Self-awareness is vital even in a decade where choice is increasingly restricted. Students have to recognise their limits. Taking a job where the possibility of failure is great is more serious now than in an age of flexibility. Students should examine how they can extend the field in which they function. This seems to be why we emphasise generic vocational skills – to allow easy transfer from one field to another.

One is attached by a field, but within it one can work at various levels, e.g., in the medical field one has a range varying from porter or ward orderly to consultant. Challenge enters guidance at this point. Motivation to avoid success undoubtedly exists, and students need to think about their willingness to strive. Field and level should form a structure for sessions in group guidance.

Jobs involve decisions. Therefore students should look at the decisions incorporated into particular occupations. Simple examples are illustrated below.

Situation 1
You are a nurse on your first night duty. A bout of influenza is decimating staff. You have two wards on which to keep an eye. Your senior colleague has gone for a meal break and will not be back for 15 minutes. Suddenly everything seems to happen. In one

ward a patient has a bout of noisy, uncontrollable vomiting, whilst in the other you have an emergency heart arrest in a patient who was apparently coping well. You had been with a terminal case in a side ward who is *in extremis* and has become conscious. You were easing her last moments. Night duty has been stressful for you – you feel tired and wretched – now this!

Assess the best way of acting in this situation. When you have come to some decision, make explicit the best principles and ethics underlying your suggestions.

Situation 2
A police sergeant is on duty in a local station one evening. Around eleven o'clock an emergency call comes in, and three officers go off in two cars to sort out the group of young people who have been reported for violence, assault on neighbours and suspected drug-taking. They are brought back to the station for questioning. The fourth one brought in is the sergeant's son, who the sergeant believed was visiting a friend in the neighbouring town.

How should the sergeant behave immediately? What should be his reactions as a policeman? How will they conflict with his role as a father?

Situation 3
The head of sixth form has had a request for a reference for a past pupil who has not obtained a job. The firm assures him that the reference will be treated as completely confidential. Due to the nature of the job precise questions are asked about honesty and reliability. The candidate was bright, hard-working, but there were several occasions on which he was suspected of dishonesty, although nothing was proved.

Should the head of sixth mention the doubts in writing? Should he ignore the suspicions and not mention them? Should he include the sentence at the end of the reference, 'If you would like further information please do not hesitate to contact me by telephone.'

After coming to a decision, justify it carefully.

Tutors can give small amounts of information about a job which are relevant to a problem. Students can be involved in the construction of such problems which are then resolved by the others in the tutor group. An extension is for partners to work together, drawing up a job description for various workers – skilled craftsmen, managerial or supervisory positions – and then devise decision-making situations.

Themes such as confidence, taking responsibility and assuming leadership should be part of the programme. One approach to this is seen in the activity set out below (sent to me by Mr John Hughes) which was devised by a group of students in a workshop at my Summer School in 1973.

Simulation: The new truck

Background brief
You are being asked to join a problem-solving situation. Assume that you are repairmen in a large business. Each day, you drive to various parts of the town to do repair work. Each of you drives a small truck and you take a pride in keeping it clean and smart. You have a possessive feeling about your truck, but naturally you would like to have a new truck when one becomes available.

The problem is that Walter Davies, the supervisor of repairs, has just heard that a new truck is to be delivered to the depot. He is not sure which of the five men under him should have the new truck, therefore he intends to let the men decide for themselves. The five men have 25 minutes in which to argue the case out.

Here are some facts about the trucks and the men in Walter Davies' crew:

George – 17 years with the company – has a 2 year-old Ford
Bill   – 11 years with the company – has a 5 year-old Morris
*John   – 10 years with the company – has a 4 year-old Ford
*Charlie – 5 years with the company – has a 3 year-old Ford
Fred   – 3 years with the company – has a 5 year-old Austin

*John and Charlie work in the suburbs and do more driving than the others.

You will be one of the people mentioned above and some further information is given on the other sheet. In acting your part accept the facts and take on the attitudes of that worker. From the beginning let your feelings develop in a natural way. When facts or events arise which are not covered by the instructions, make up things which are in line with real life.

Walter Davies
He has heard that this new truck is available. He has to decide who should have it – often there are hard feelings, because each member seems to think he is entitled to the new truck, and he finds it hard to be fair. As a matter of fact, it turns out that, whatever he decided, most of the men consider it wrong. The new truck is an Austin. Walter Davies plays no part because he has handed the problem over to the repairmen.

Bill
You feel you deserve a new truck. Your present truck is old, and since the more senior man has a fairly new truck, you should get this one. You have taken excellent care of your present Morris and have kept it looking like new. A man deserves to be rewarded if he treats a company truck as he would his own.

Fred
You have the poorest truck in the group. It is 5 years old, and before you got it the truck had been in a bad smash. It has never been good, and you have put up with it for three years. It's about time you had a good truck to drive, and you feel the next one should be yours. You have a good accident record. The only accident you had was when you hit the door of Charlie's truck when he opened it as you were backing out of the garage. You hope the truck is a Ford, since you prefer them.

George
When a new Austin truck becomes available, you think you should have it because, after all, you have been with the firm longest. You don't like your present truck. Your own car is an Austin and you prefer an Austin truck, such as you had before you got the Ford.

Charlie
The heater in your present truck is inadequate. Since Fred backed into the door of your truck it has never been repaired to fit right. The door lets in too much cold air, and you get colds and chills from this. You want a warm truck as you have lots of driving to do. As long as it has good tyres, brakes and is comfortable, you don't care about its make.

John
Your truck is in good condition mechanically, but the paint-work is poor. As you work in the suburbs where the customers are better off, you feel it presents a poor image of the firm. You keep your overalls clean and try to present a picture of efficiency, but resent your shabby truck. If you don't get the truck, you think Charlie should have the new truck and so you will support him.

> Post-play discussion is crucial. Ways of coping and reactions are identified and then evaluated. The following mechanisms appear:
>
> — making an implicit bargain with a fellow worker that, if you support him, you will gain some advantage, e.g., get rid of your truck and have his which is better;
>
> — blind blocking of others when you realise you are not getting the truck;

> - blaming the foreman, saying it is his job to make the decision;
> - making a coalition which attacks and demoralises the man with the strongest case.

Excellent material can be found in Hopson and Hopson (1973) and the School Council Careers Education and Guidance Project, Work 2 and Work 3. The materials emanating from CRAC are also valuable.

The part played by a sense of being in control or feeling a pawn is of interest. Is the world seen as full of hostile pressures or does the student believe he can find a way to achieve what he desires? Working from fear of failure has to be identified and closely examined. This means that the individual is working to avoid guilt, shame or punishment. Fear of disapproval is part of being human, but it makes for passivity and superficiality. What is meant by success, what success the individual finds meaningful and how success can be obtained in this age provide the material for a number of sessions.

Again, reference can be made to predictions and the way they shape behaviour. Perhaps the constructive tough-mindedness of guidance emerges as we discuss issues of self-fulfilment. Guidance does not eliminate anxiety – it helps students use it constructively. Eventually we have to choose between anxiety, as we strive realistically to be the best that we can be even in difficult conditions, or guilt and shame stemming from the realisation that we denied ourselves the chance of self-realisation.

5: Group interaction and social skills

Summary points

1. Standpoint-taking is an essential skill in the development of social competence. Social anxiety centres on fear of loss of control, fear of the limelight and dislike of making an adverse impression on authority figures. Audience anxiety is particularly significant in the 16-19 year-old and should be considered carefully in the guidance programme. The vulnerability of the students and the importance of the issues have to be taken into account. The methods used by tutors should neither trivialise or encourage over-simplification of reality, nor should they violate personal space. Students need help to learn to discriminate between situations, and to detect alternative constructive strategies of coping.

2. Reactions to frustration, loss of face and negative predictions of outcomes of behaviour are key issues in students' lives and therefore in guidance. Students have to learn to identify, and then to act differently at trigger points, i.e., the point of provocation which instigates negative behaviour.
Understanding of the power of predictions on those who feel pawns is examined as a way of increasing students' personal autonomy.

3. Leadership is examined as a topic of major concern to the age group. Encouragement is offered to analyse leadership as a bargaining process in which power largely rests with the followers. Rotter's *Social Learning Theory* helpfully draws attention to the situation as a major factor in understanding group interaction, although individual preferences for a particular role or type of reinforcement are seen as important. Other mechanisms such as pairing have to be understood and are discussed.

4. Students need to recognise the factors which erode individual responsibility, and which also contribute to increased risk in group-based decisions. Comprehension of such forces is necessary for the maintenance of personal integrity.

Sense and sensitivity for the tutor
Guidance is concerned with creating awareness in students of their self-diminishing behaviours, providing the opportunity to assess the standpoints of others, and to develop skills of problem-solving. Tutors should try to give students intellectual and practical tools for development, avoiding the threat which comes from approaches which are too rigid or too unstructured.

Trust versus mistrust is a theme to which the tutor is sensitive. We can assume trust, but at the same time we may be offering guidance which imposes solutions. The 16 - 19 year-old reacts by generating an artificial self which hides the inner anxiety. Such guidance is ineffective, perhaps harmful. Most young people simply ignore it as irrelevant. Group counselling using the structure suggested in Chapter 3 can help students examine:

Themes for group counselling focused on social interaction
1. The reasons for rejection of certain aspects of school, college or training course.
2. Aspects of people or positions to which students respond with enthusiasm or caution.
3. Ways of coping with 'Don't do as I do; do as I say' attitudes.
4. Learning to cope with the hypocrisy of obeying things to which they are not committed as a necessary response, e.g., College rules.
5. Differentiation between people with whom you can be honest and spontaneous and those with whom you have to establish more limited or guarded relationships.

Students are trapped into situations where contradictory or 'double-bind' forces exist. The students see a certain job as highly desirable; *but* if they show they care too obviously about it they feel loss of face when they don't get it; *but* they may also lose face if they don't try to get it. Action involves risk. To seek a job may bring confirmation that one is not going to get one. A sense of exposure is created by the decision to look for the job, and a sense of blame by the decision not to.

Group guidance opens up these possibilities which bedevil young people.

Communication skills
I have found the following exercise useful with 16 - 18 year-olds,

provided that the objectives are carefully explained, the structure emphasised and follow-up discussion is given sufficient time.

A communication exercise

Objectives
'We send messages to people in many ways. Even our bodies send messages – we can stand aggressively or passively. Facial expressions, voices and eye contact all play a part. It is helpful to think about the way we communicate as part of our success in life. You will not be asked to touch anyone or do anything embarrassing. I shall tell you when to do something else or discuss.'

Structure
The tutor maintains strict control of the session, modifying the times suggested to match what is happening.

Activity
Students work in groups of four. Ensure each small group is a fair distance from any other.

1. Ask the students to discuss the kind of person they feel they can talk to easily. (*Allow 5 minutes.*)
2. Tutor stops groups and asks them if they found it easy to talk about the topic.
   The group then discusses this for a few moments.
3. Tutor asks them to discuss the situations where they find it difficult to say what they want. (*Allow 5-7 minutes.*)
4. Tutor intervenes, asking how it went. A little feedback is given.
5. In each group partners tell one another about their impression of the other's style of communication. The tutor illustrates, 'For example, does he seem confident, smile or pay attention to what the other person says?' (*Allow 6 minutes.*)
6. They then return to the group of four and discuss the qualities of the person who makes others want to listen to him. (*Allow 5 minutes.*)
7. In each small group a different partner is chosen. In silence, they are asked to stand up and make eye contact until one of them breaks it. They stand about 2 feet away from one another. (*About 3 minutes are necessary.*)
8. Discussion in the small group follows. The tutor introduces the idea of dominance, – embarrassment when one catches someone's eye in the train; or the awkwardness of getting past someone on the pavement when eye contact has been made, since both move in the same direction until the contact is broken. Feelings about people making eye contact as you talk can be discussed. (*Allow 10 minutes.*)

9. Tell them to imagine they have lost all power of speech, but have to send an important message and reply non-verbally, using hands, legs, facial expression, etc. (*Allow 4 minutes.*)
10. Small group discussion about the way they use their hands or faces when talking to people. How do they feel when someone has a blank face or never smiles as they talk to him or her. Embarrassment can be examined. (*Allow 8 minutes.*)
11. Tutor gets feedback from whole tutor group; emphasises points made about effective communication, showing that it has been a learning experience.

Some students lack listening skills and have to be convinced of their importance. Tutors can relate these skills to learning, success in a job, or getting on with people. The following exercise can be most useful, provided that the speaker chooses his own topic.

A listening exercise

Objective
To produce awareness of the skills involved in listening and to provide practice in listening and recall.

Step 1
Write the following list on the board:
- Sit still.
- Don't interrupt.
- Give signs that you are interested.
- Keep eye contact.
- Respond by nodding or making approving sounds.
- Look at the speaker.
- Don't criticise.
- When the speaker stops, encourage him to develop what he has been saying.
- Help when the speaker seems lost for words.

Students are asked to use the ladder technique to rank the skills in ascending order of importance. They then justify their rank order with a partner. The object is to allow them to think rather than to suggest there is one correct order.

Step 2
Triads are formed. One person chooses a topic in which he is interested. Another listens. The third is an observer who uses the list of skills to make notes on the quality of listening. After 15 minutes or so the listener tells speaker and observer what was

said. Both then comment on the accuracy of the listener's performance, being as helpful as possible. (This exercise should be demanding, hence the emphasis on a topic in which the speaker is interested, and a fairly long speaking time.)

Communication is affected by the reactions of friends. Young people, however, do not necessarily find the support of friends helpful in coming to a decision. This is especially true when they tend to gain identity through opposition. The following exercises are typical of those which may be developed.

To surf or swot

Objective
To provide practice in communication under conditions of opposition and support.

Activity
Groups of four discuss the topic below.

It is two weeks before the examinations. The weather is glorious and seems settled for the next few days. Bill is a keen surfer, and decides that he might as well enjoy himself and go surfing. He knows he will probably get the results he needs if he revises thoroughly – his performance in the class is marginal. But the sun has rarely shone this summer.

Step 1
One student takes the role of Bill. The other three are friends who oppose his viewpoint and attempt to refute his arguments.
(*Allow 8-10 minutes.*)

Step 2
The same student plays Bill, but this time his friends support him and encourage him.

Step 3
The small groups then discuss whether it is easier to come to a decision when friends oppose or support one. The issue of differences in the type of decision reached can be broached, e.g., does opposition lead you to make up your mind early on, and to refuse to modify your decision?

Is it worth it?

Objectives and *procedures* are as before. The situation is:

Mark is on a sixth-form course for which there is no payment. His parents have been giving him £5 pocket money. He lands a job at a

> supermarket on Saturdays which brings him in £12. His parents react by cutting his pocket money to £1. Mark feels bitter. He feels his initiative is being punished, so he decides it will be better to stay in bed on Saturdays.

There is a tendency for pastoral care and guidance to use too many questionnaires. The occasional questionnaire, however, is a helpful tool. The one set out below makes a good basis for group counselling discussion or small group work. It would be counter-productive to use it as a class lesson in which individuals have to answer questions.

> ## Communication and learning
>
> We can all relate to other people more productively. Inter-personal communication is important in many careers. It will help you to look at the issues raised in this questionnaire, and to discuss their implications with a trusted friend.
>
> Be clear that this guidance questionnaire is for your eyes only, and not for your tutor. You will be given the opportunity to discuss what you want with a selected friend. It will not lead to interrogation!
> (The blank spaces are not shown in this outline form.)
>
> *One*
> Think of a time recently when you found it easy to admit you were wrong. Describe it below.
> – Now think of a situation when you would find it hard to admit you were in the wrong. Details can go below.
> – Try to explain the reasons for the difference.
>
> *Two*
> Are there times when you find it hard to let others known that you do not know the answer? If so, jot them down. Then try to explain what makes it hard to admit lack of knowledge.
>
> *Three*
> All of us tend to put up a bit of a 'front' with people in authority.
> – When does this happen to you?
> – What form does the 'front' take?
> – Why do you think this happens to you?
>
> *Four*
> When do you feel that, however hard you try, the other person will not understand you?

> *Five*
> We all need to put on an act sometimes.
> - When does this happen to you?
> - What does it do to communication between you and others?
>
> *Six*
> All of us feel a little uncomfortable at times when the limelight turns on us and everyone seems to be watching. How do you cope?
>
> *Seven*
> We can all say the wrong thing. We can also give a wrong impression of ourselves, not by what we say, but by
> - the way we say it;
> - the way we sit or stand;
> - our facial expression;
> - the way we move.
>
> Make a few notes about the ways in which this happens to you.

The tutor must refrain from questioning. Discussion should be in small groups. At the end of the guidance session the tutor shows the ubiquity of these tendencies and reinforces the fact that they are remediable. Such areas cannot be avoided, for the frequent lament of many 16 - 19 year-olds is, 'Why do things go sour on me?' or, 'Why can't I put myself across as I really am?' The involvement of students in the selection of situations and the development of activities ensures that a joint learning process develops.

Tension management and social competence
My emphasis on student involvement in negotiation of content affirms that mechanistic approaches or recipes will not work. Such techniques feed the students' unrealistic expectations in teachers, leading to ultimate rejection because the promises of a simple answer were not met. *School and After* (1978) raises the basic question whether schools are to prepare pupils for the realities of what follows or to protect them from it for as long as possible. The latter position in untenable. Provision of knowledge about ways of coping with stress and the fostering of cognitive skills can be, as suggested by the researchers cited in Chapter 1, a sensible form of preparation. The emphasis on learning in a controlled context minimises inhibitory anxiety and the erection of defences.

Realism suggests that even so we cannot take it for granted that what is learned will be transferred to other areas of students' lives. Current work in moral development focuses on identification and clarification of issues, sharpening the precision of reasoning and stimulating standpoint – taking ability, e.g., Lickona (Ed.) (1976) and Ward (Ed.) (1982). Moral education can be related to concrete dilemmas from which principles can be extracted, e.g., 'If you saw a crime being committed would you report it?' Issues of interference, responsibility and response to distress emerge. Even the allegedly less able student can reason cogently about such considerations when they are embedded in concrete, familiar situations.

Discussion of the pervasiveness of social anxiety, its normality and ways of coping form the initial step. Buss (1980) provides a fund of knowledge for the tutor. The examination of audience anxiety follows. This has two major components:

1 Anxiety about evaluation, which incorporates fear of failure.
2 Anxiety about being rejected as a person. (The 16 - 19 age group tends to take criticism personally and be unduly sensitive to blame.)

Worthwhile insights can be provided by comparisons of audience anxiety where the setting is:

1 Familiar, and friends are involved.
2 Unfamiliar, and involving persons of high status, e.g., a tribunal or selection panel.

Next, the tutor might ask students to detect and consider situations in which they feel social objects:

1 Being approached accusingly by a drunk in a busy street.
2 Entering a department store at a slack period and feeling the focus of the eyes of bored assistants.
3 A girl walking past a group of soldiers or a boy walking past a group of 'skins'.
4 Stripping in the presence of others for a shower after exercise or in hospital.

Reactions to public scrutiny are illuminating, e.g.:

1 Fear of making a speech error on a formal occasion.
2 Forgetting someone's name or title.
3 Coping with being the object of laughter or ridicule.

Major themes to be explored

1 Reactions to frustration in public settings.
2 Coping with embarrassment.

3 Fear of being caught in the limelight.
4 Making adverse impressions on authority figures.
5 Positive presentation of self.
6 Social issues associated with stereotypes of masculinity and feminity.
7 Co-operative behaviours.

The following cartoons have stimulated discussion.

FEAR OF LOSING CONTROL

FEAR OF THE LIMELIGHT

FEAR OF REVEALING INADEQUACY

STRANGERS

WHAT IS SHE LIKE?

WHAT IS HE LIKE?

INTIMATES

AM I ACCEPTABLE?

Anxieties about relationships

THE BODILY SELF

(thought: AM I NORMAL... ATTRACTIVE?)

FEELINGS FANTASIES

Anxieties about oneself

EXAMINATION ANXIETY

Examination anxiety

Small group discussion on embarrassment arising in certain situations forms the next step.
1 Someone watching you when you are working at a machine or writing. Feelings when the invigilator stands behind you in an examination.
2 Being the focus for a practical joke when surrounded by people you don't know.
3 Going out for the evening and then finding you are dressed differently from everyone else.
4 Clumsiness in public, e.g., inadvertently knocking over someone's drink at the bar when it is not crowded.
5 Telling a dirty joke which is received in stony silence.

A useful ploy is to take these situations and ask small groups of three or four students to:
1. Tease out why they are embarrassing, perhaps stressful.
2. Work out *several* possible ways of coping.
3. Find a parallel situation and turn it into a decision-making exercise.
4. Present their findings on the original situation to the whole tutor group.
5. Give the group the decision-making exercise.
6. Collect feedback and lead the discussion.

Teaching social skills: The tutor's approach

The ideas suggested stem from development of an activity formulated by experienced teachers receiving full-time university-based training in 1972/73. Theory and research presented in my lectures on simulations, games and the development of standpoint-taking were translated into practical activities. During the years I have developed this further in my work, but I would like to acknowledge their initiative.

This teaching approach can be developed from a simple form into more complex activities as tutors gain confidence. The first two steps are:
1. Presentation of situations centred on any combination of the following, to be discussed by small groups:
   - frustration;
   - criteria for trust;
   - trigger situations which cause aggression and escalation of disruptive behaviour;
   - consensus about a decision within the group;
   - pressure from peers;
   - challenge to masculinity or femininity;
   - loss of face/prestige;
   - coping with ridicule;
   - unwanted comparisons;
   - resistance to the temptation to indulge in negative behaviour;
   - changing one's mind;
   - competition;
   - scape-goating and other group processes.
2. Each group has a peer judge, who acts as a source of credible comment and evaluation, using guide-lines suggested by the tutor.

Peer judge notes

Instructions
1. When the group has made its decision, please say what you think of it, honestly but helpfully. Look at any strengths and weaknesses.
2. DO NOT JOIN IN THE DISCUSSION WHEN THEY ARE WORKING OUT WHAT THEY WOULD DO. MAKE NOTES FOR YOUR EVALUATION.
3. The following will help:
   a. Do you feel they are tackling the situation honestly?
   b. Do you think they are leaving important things out? If so, note this. Draw attention to it later.
   c. Try to find out what is shaping their ideas and statements, e.g., what their friends might say, being tough, or comparing themselves with other people.
   d. Do you think their decision is too risky or not challenging enough?
   e. Is one person dominating the group, making up other people's minds, or influencing others?
   f. Do you think there is a better decision? If so, please tell them.
   g. Do you see snags or problems they have ignored? If so, please talk about it.
   h. Their decision may sound good, but do you believe they would do what they suggest in real life? Discuss this with them, if you feel it worth while.

With regard to peer judges, two possibilities are open to you. In each round or situation you can either have the same peer judge or allow each member in turn to evaluate decisions.

The activities are directed by the tutor as follows:
   a. Groups of four are formed, with a fifth person as a peer judge.
   b. The groups discuss the situation generally for 12 - 15 minutes.
   c. They are then given 10 minutes in which to make a decision based on the final question presented on paper and tape.
   d. The peer judge evaluates the decision and makes general comments to his group.
   e. The tutor then has a general discussion with the total tutor group, ending with a clear summary of what has been learned.

Situations – Level 1

1 *Frustration*
You are four friends who are avid soccer fans. Your great ambition

has been to attend the Cup Final as the team you have supported faithfully has crashed its way through to Wembley. By a minor miracle one of you gets three tickets, but there are no more. Fathers, relations and friends have tried everywhere for you, to no avail. A letter to the team produces sympathy but no ticket. You can't afford the touts' monstrous prices – even if you could, the risk is too great. Forged tickets have been detected.

How would you cope with this situation without leaving someone feeling bad? You have always prided yourselves on your good sense and maturity.

2 *Falsely accused*

The four of you have been at a pop festival for the weekend. You slept in dormitories in a hostel, and pilfering occurred. Quite a lot of money was taken during the night from people's wallets. It was lucky none of you lost anything, because one of you took a foolishly large sum of money. You are all in the station buffet, and the one with the money is buying the others a drink. A yell rends the air: 'That's the one, Jim! I saw him go over to your bunk about 2.00 a.m. and pick up your anorak. That's the thief! Now he's getting rid of the lolly.' Everybody looks at you. The other group – also four in number – advances.

What is the best way of dealing with the situation?

3 *Embarrassment*

The latest sex and violence film has hit the town. Most people in your age group have seen it. Unfortunately, you had to ask your parents for cash when your best friend came round. This meant explaining why. Father blew up, but then calmed down and said he'd come with you both and then it would be 'off your chest'. Your mother's response was, 'Over my dead body – no daughter of mine is going to such filth.' Your friend is angry at all this – you also know she thinks you lack the strength to stand up for yourself.

What is the most constructive way of dealing with this situation? Justify your decision.

4 *Falsely accused*

The four of you are in the pub. One of you is under age, although he doesn't look it. The barman politely accuses him of not paying for his drink. Despite the politeness and, although he is under age, your friend reacts to the mistake by getting very angry. The barman is then convinced he hasn't paid for it. The others know he has paid, but also know that the accused friend has a problem with his temper –

once roused he won't stop for anybody. One of you did try to pay again for the drink to stop trouble, but your friend would not allow that. The police station is literally two minutes away. There is someone in the bar from your friend's road who doesn't like him and who knows how old he is.

How can things be kept under control?

5 *Boasting and loss of face*
One of you tends to brag – somehow he can't stop it. As he's basically all right you put up with it. In fact, if you pull his leg and make him laugh, he usually stops. He doesn't seem to appreciate that he upsets others, and that they are less kind than you. He has just alienated a number of people by boasting that he will get a particularly prestigious electronics apprenticeship. The results come through and he has failed. Now he has to face the sarcasm of those he has upset. A group comes up to the four of you at break intent on putting him through it.

What is the best way of coping? Remember he has plenty of enemies already.

6 *Challenge to masculinity*
You are all at the disco, but one of you is not having great success with the girls. The trouble is that he predicts that if he asks a girl for a dance or a date she'll turn him down. This makes him confused and uncertain, and he appears 'wet'. The group is going out tomorrow – the others have firm girl friends. They encourage him to ask a girl to come with him tomorrow night. The worst happens. She laughs and makes fun of him, saying, so that the other boys and girls can hear, 'Where have you crawled out from? What will my friends say if I go out with a wet like you? They'll think I'm desperate. No thanks, mini-man!' The boys with her suggest he goes back to Mum – she'll be looking for him soon.

How can you preserve dignity and self-respect in this situation?

7 *Trust*
It's near Christmas. One of you has just lost his job. You meet in the club where he shows embarrassment because he can't pay for his round. You all reassure him. Then he goes on to say that he's in a spot of trouble because he bought a stereo-cassette recorder cheap but he can't pay for it. The bloke expects the cash, £30, tonight – and he's tough. Will you lend him the £30. You are all in work – it's a tenner each. You can manage it, but will you trust him?

What considerations would you use to make up your minds?

8 *Peer pressures and incitement to delinquency*
John bought a record-player on Monday for the small voluntary youth group, to which you do not belong. The members contributed towards it. John tells you that when he was wiring it up, somehow he knocked it off the corner of the table on to the concrete, with disastrous results. Next day he met the manager of the shop from which he bought it, who said, 'Drop in tomorrow and insure it.' 'Too late,' said John gloomily. 'The thing's broken because I was careless.' The manager replied 'Don't worry! I'll put the date of purchase as tomorrow when you pay me the premium. It covers accident, so we'll wait a week and then claim.' John is honest in most ways, and he was doubtful. His fellow club members thought it was a good idea, saying he would be daft not to do it. Anyway, they either wanted their money back or a record-player that worked.

What should John do? Give reasons.

9 *Consensus under pressure of time*
You are all at the disco when the DJ tells you that your group can have a record played and be named. This happens only once on Saturday evening, so being asked gives you the prestige of being recognised as 'regulars'. The DJ gives you 12 minutes to make up your mind, saying you must all agree. He's had trouble before. To your surprise, Dave, who is usually co-operative, digs his heels in at once, saying he will only have The Animals' latest, which the others detest.

How do you deal with this?

10 *Misreading a situation*
Three of you have been active in the peace movement. You attend local meetings and rallies, which are orderly and well-conducted. You convince Steve that he ought to come – this is his first time. His parents are elderly, strict, and out of touch with youth. They over-protect him, so they let him come with reluctance.

Trouble-makers have infiltrated, and for the first time fights develop. The disrupters are vicious, and Steve gets attacked. The police actually rescue him from the bully-boys. You are taking him home with a badly torn shirt, black eye and bloody nose when a car stops. It is Steve's parents, who have been shopping. They get out and berate you all, blaming you for leading Steve into trouble. This is too much for Bob, who was attacked himself, so he yells, 'You stupid old geriatrics!'

How does one cope with this?

11 *Changing one's mind*
The four of you had decided to spend five days in the Pennines in the summer. Routes had been planned, equipment bought and arrangements made to link up with a group of friends at the end. Jim suddenly gets doubtful about the whole thing and wants to opt out. The others are furious, feeling that Jim has conned them.

What is the most sensible way for them to act?

12 *Body image*
The four of you have been friends since the primary school. Paul is a bit unusual physically: he has a slight squint, he walks rather clumsily – and from his viewpoint the worst thing is that he is short and slight. He's fine with you, but he tends to be aggressive with others, running his life on the principle of, 'Get them before they get you.' You all back him up, but other people dislike you because of him. You wish he didn't have to make so much trouble. You know that his feelings about his appearance and physique are partly responsible for his behaviour. After a particularly difficult incident in which he involved you all, you decide something has to be done.

How would you approach the problem?

13 *The limits to membership of a group*
You are at the disco. It is near the end of the evening. You have enjoyed yourselves, but one of you hasn't danced all night: the others in the group want to make him dance.

Because you find a group attractive, do you have to do everything the group wants you to do? Does the group have the right to make him dance?

14 *After-the-event justifications for behaviour*
You all went to the Youth Club, but Molly behaved abominably to Sheila, who is another member of her own age. She was incredibly hostile and rude and the three of you were embarrassed. On the way

9 The 'yes-man', who always agrees, but this makes one doubt arguments. You all know that the real reason is that Molly likes a boy who prefers Sheila.

Do you let her get away with this?

Situations – Level 2
The situations we have seen concern young people because they often cannot cope well with them. After some experience, the learning can be sharpened by giving positions or standpoints from which students argue; positions which incorporate behaviour strategies. The

position taken by students is varied systematically, which makes them look at problems from different viewpoints. Roles commonly taken up in groups are used, e.g.

1. The social-emotional leader, i.e., the person who is quick to pour oil on troubled water and can repair damaged relationships.
2. The cynic, ie. the person who pours cold water on ideas and questions motives.
3. The 'Blow you, Jack. I'm all right!' type, who thinks of himself only.
4. The one who goes along passively with the majority decisions.
5. The manipulator, who indirectly persuades others to do what he wants.
6. The clown, who uses joking to cover his own anxieties and acquire acceptability.
7. The scapegoat, who collects all the blame.
8. The superior 'putter-down' of others.
9. The 'yes-man', who always agrees, but this makes one doubt his honesty.
10. The martyr, who relinquishes his own ideas and desires, accepting those of others with patience.
11. The 'life and soul of the party', who irritates and exhausts everybody.
12. The 'blackmailer', who reminds you of the past and what he has done.

This list is not exhaustive – students should be encouraged to extend it. In exploring the situation students must choose a specified standpoint from those given on a flip chart or overhead projector. The idea is illustrated in relation to two of the situations in Level 1.

---

5 *Boasting and loss of face*

1	CLOWN	You are the one who boasted. You have learned you can sometimes wriggle out of these situations by making a joke against yourself.
2	SUPPORTIVE SOCIAL-EMOTIONAL LEADER	You are a good friend of the bragger. You recognise his faults, but he is a good mate. You think it will be best to be honest, admitting he does these things, but you appeal to the others decency, asking them to appreciate his feelings.

| 3 MANIPULATOR | You are a bit fed up with the bragger, but you don't let anyone know that you feel it is time he had a lesson. You begin with a remark calculated to rebound on him because it irritates the opposition. 'Well, you're just jealous because none of you is as good as he is.' |

It will be helpful to let individuals discuss their standpoints, sharing ideas before the argument begins. Support will be needed at the first attempt. A trial run for three or four minutes is profitable. Distinguish clearly between the standpoint-taking and the decision-making.

13 *The limits to membership of a group*

1 AGGRESSIVE/COERCIVE	You decide to push this. You ask, 'Why should he come along, and then not do the same as the rest of us?'
2 SOCIAL-EMOTIONAL LEADER	You suspect strong feelings could spoil a good evening. You decide the best thing will be to change the situation by going to the bar and getting cokes for everybody.
3 THE YES-MAN	You don't want trouble. You'll agree with whoever seems to be winning the argument.
4 THE MARTYR	You are the one who hasn't danced. You suppose that once again you'll have to do what they want. You will, however, protest before you do.

A caution

Students need to practice this taking of standpoints, so immediate good results are unlikely. Their background has often made them prisoners of a rigid egocentricity. It is helpful to get four who are interested in drama to improvise, taping the result as an illustration for others. When he presents the introductory tape the tutor emphasizes the desirability of standpoint-taking.

This book has stressed thinking and verbalisation as the core of experiential learning in guidance. If guidance *is* to be a joint learning experience, students should be allowed to detect situations of concern, construct simulations and evaluate coping strategies. I have often told them they are not the passive recipients of my non-wisdom. Learning is about life, and they are living now. Tutors therefore should encourage them to think about factors such as threat in their lives. Deutsch (1973) shows that threats in social interaction have a profound effect on co-operation – scarcely surprising – but young adults need to consider the implications of his findings that co-operation under threat is interpreted as weakness. They may also need to consider Milgram's (1974) findings that trust in expert authority can over-ride other values. Who are the experts for them and what are their credentials?

Co-operation is both an attitude and a skill. Over-stress of the personality aspects of attitudes ignores the fact that attitudes are learned and have functions for their holders. Failure to see this blocks development. To focus on attitudes as psychological characteristics rather than as social relationships means we ignore the teaching of behavioural skills. Even at 16 - 19, many individuals have a limited repertoire of skills – hence we may need to teach co-operation.

In *Teaching Study Skills* (1981) I found it useful to examine the relationship between co-operation and competition. They are not mutually exclusive. Self-help groups can be developed in which students co-operate to compete more effectively in public examinations. Partner and small group co-operation should be integral to the education of this age group. Tutors setting co-operative tasks should discuss the goals with students so that they can assess their achievement.

In *Teaching Study Skills* we have seen the importance of learning about learning, including verbalisation of strategies. Similarly, students learning co-operative skills should look at:

1 Orientation to the co-operative task.
2 Evaluation and provision of mutual feedback after the task.

Orientation

1 What *exactly* do we have to achieve?
2 What steps do we have to take?

3 Division of labour – who can do what best?
4 Do we need a leader? If so, what does he do?
5 How can we collect good ideas?
6 Do we listen to one another?
7 How can we improve our performance this time?

Feedback and self-evaluation

1 What strengths have we got as a group working together? How can we build on them?
2 In what ways do we need to improve our planning?
3 What do we need to do to improve our performance next time? What mistakes did we make?
4 How satisfied are we with what we achieved?

Greater understanding of co-operation can be induced by simple exercises such as the Youth Club Dance. The tutor should discuss confrontations, bargaining, and the feelings likely to arise in such a meeting which create barriers to planning.

Youth Club Dance

1 *Objective of simulation*
To develop skills in co-operation, bargaining and standpoint-taking.

2 *Instructions to participants*
You will be one of the people described below, so choose your character and in the meeting put forward the views you think that person will hold, using the information given. (If the discussion leads on to a topic about which your 'sketch' does not help you, say what you think your person would say in that situation.)

You have 40 minutes to cover the points listed. If more time is needed, another meeting will have to be arranged for tomorrow. This will be difficult for Jim and Anne.

3 *Background brief*
You are attending a Youth Club Committee meeting to organise a dance. Tom, the leader, has outlined an agenda. The things to be decided are:
   a What age group should be allowed in?
   b The type of music to be played.
   c What food and drink should be made available?
   d Whether smoking should be allowed.

>   e What type of lighting to have?
>   f What time the club dance starts and finishes?
>   g Should there be an entrance fee, and, if so, how much?
>
> *Here are some facts about the people taking part.*
>
> *Tom* – The club leader. He is concerned that the dance should involve as many people connected with the club as possible. He is keen on preserving the club's good image, and indeed in improving it, as he has received a letter of complaint from local residents about noise at a previous club event. He would like the times to be from 7.30 p.m. until 10.30 p.m., and wishes to keep everything legal and safe. He has a fairly easy-going attitude to smoking, but wants to limit drinking to coffee and squash. He thinks a fee should be charged, although the funds would allow them to run it free.
>
> *Jim* – aged 18. He feels strongly that the dance should be a more grown-up affair, that alcoholic drinks should be available for those legally able to buy them. He would like the event to continue to 1.00 a.m. He thinks that a fee should be charged, but does not feel strongly about this. As far as he is concerned, the music should be exclusively 'soul'.
>
> *Sally* – aged 16. She wants to keep in with the leader, but does not want too many younger members there. She thinks the dance should be for 16 year-olds and upwards, and that non-members should be admitted. She would like dim, coloured lighting effects.
>
> *Robert* – aged 14. He is interested in a lot of food and loud 'disco' music and he is an Ultra Vox fan. He thinks that admission should be free and he is very anti-smoking.
>
> *Anne* – aged 13. She wants only crisps and coke to be available and is not fussy about the type of music. She is hoping that 'new' boys will come, so wants it to be open to non-members.

Group interaction

This is a practical exposition, rather than a theoretical survey of group processes. Lack of understanding of group interaction in terms meaningful to the individual means that there is little possibility of modifying constricting behaviours.

Let us begin with judgements of others. Rommetweit (1960) showed that identification of a single salient characteristic was sufficient to trigger off a sequence of automatic responses which were rarely questioned. Similar tendencies appeared in Asch's (1946) work on impression formation. The power of initial impressions in shaping reactions, and the validity of such judgements should be given high priority in guidance.

In evaluation of style of interaction, Rotter *et al* (1972) have much to offer. Personality is *not* viewed solely as a set of internalised characteristics carried by the individual from situation to situation: it is seen as a set of potentials for responding to many types of social situations. It is learned and open to modification. Inadequate as this description of it is, this theory raises questions which form a good introduction to group interaction. Guidance sessions should encourage students to examine the key themes below:

Key themes in group interaction

1 Which behaviours are likely to appear or not appear in different situations?
2 What reward or punishment do students expect in specific situations?
  How is this related to previous experience?
3 How do students think that their beliefs about what will occur affect their behaviour in groups?
4 Which roles do they prefer or tend to take up in different group situations?

It has been useful to ask students to direct these questions to three different group situations they consider important, e.g.
– leisure time activity;
– family;
– class and learning situations.

Students will probably find themselves questioning their behaviours and recognising erroneous expectations. It is at this point that the group counselling techniques of Chapter 3 are essential. Readers may be surprised at the emphasis on specific situations, yet people are reliable in some contexts and not in others. Most of us have met the adolescent who is a devil at home but an angel in the classroom, or the reverse.

Students should actively select situations and problems. This presents little difficulty if the *rapport* and trust that is essential for good tutoring has been created. Situations within the Sixth-Form Common Room, discussion groups, part-time work, the disco and sport can be examined in the light of the above.

Based on painstaking research, Bales (1970) produced a three-dimensional model of group interaction. Power, attraction and adherence to the basic values of the group are highlighted.

Taking different group situations, students can ask, 'In this group do I tend to –
1 be dominant or submissive?
2 arouse pleasant or hostile feelings in others?
3 help or hinder achievement of the group task, reject or accept the values which mark it?'

Kelly's (1955) character-sketch technique provides useful material for understanding behaviour in groups. The instructions would be:

Write about yourself in important group situations. Write as if you were somebody else – somebody who knows you even better than your best friend does. Try to be as understanding of yourself as possible. To make sure you write about yourself as an observer, begin in the third person, e.g., John prefers to take the role - - -, *or*, Susan is the kind of girl - - -.

It is important that students understand that these essays are for their own sight *only*, for future use in guidance sessions. Analysis takes the form of:

1 Assessing strengths and areas where the student feels change is desirable.
2 Looking for ways of developing strengths and initiating change.
3 Extracting qualities/behaviours that merit discussion, e.g. humour, forcefulness, enthusiasm or sympathy.
4 Answering the questions:
'What feelings do I have? Why?'
'What roles do I take up? What is the result?'

Discussion of performance in group situations can occur with trusted peers of their choice. Some specific area of group interaction can be taken by the student for closer examination. Targets are then set. The tutor uses a behavioural approach, employing the principle of 'one step at a time, and the easiest one first'.

Systematic understanding of group interaction is made easier by:

1 Exploring the salient characteristics of those who function well in certain group situations and comparing them with those of ineffective ones.
2 Observing – Who speaks?
   – To whom do they speak?
   – What response does their message evoke? For example, welcomed, ignored, not taken seriously?
   – Who takes control? In which situations and with what results?

The above involves discussion within the accepting climate produced through group counselling. There is a worrying tendency for guidance to fluctuate between over-reliance on role play and the over-use of check lists and questionnaires. Tapes can be used to extend the repertoire of behaviours. Many 16 - 19 year-olds retain a measure of 'identity by opposition'. This apparently negative state of affairs can be used to foster development. Many students brush off advice, but they are prepared to criticise. This can be harnessed. An example is given below.

Coping with the joker

Tape

Bill found himself the object of Len's practical jokes, which were often far from funny. They had become increasingly unpleasant over the last month. So Bill decided to think out the situation. First, he realised that he showed Len he felt confused and angry. Next, he often made a feeble remark which Len seized on and used to make the others laugh at him even more. When Bill lost his temper and hit out it made things worse. The others seemed to lose any sympathy for him when it occurred. Something had to be done! Bill decided to take the following steps:

   1 Not to give Len his pay-off by showing confusion or being feeble. He would laugh and say. 'If it helps you – good!' Then he would move away and talk to someone with whom he got on reasonably well.

   2 He would work to build up his position in the group, joining in things more. All this he would do with as little fuss as possible.

Tutor's instructions

   'Now listen again, taking notes. Criticise Bill's ideas, showing better ways of tackling the problem. Is there anything he has left out?

   'When you have done this, discuss your ideas with two other friends. Compare notes.'

The life-space diagram can be used (Hamblin, 1974). A modification of Landfield's (1969) construct technique has yielded good results with those of average or above average intelligence. The objective is to help the student become more aware of his social language and the idiosyncratic ways in which he evaluates people in social situations.

Instructions

   1 The paper is laid out as below. The student is told to think about the chosen characteristic which is related to successful interaction. To ensure that it is relevant to his life he is told to think of a person who has that characteristic.

Liked by members of a group
Fill in each box in the order indicated by the numbers.

1 What is the most important quality of the person who is liked by members of a group?	2 What kind of person is *not* liked by members of a group? Write down the most important thing about this kind of person.
3 Write some more about the kind of person who is liked by others in a group.	4 What more would you like to say about a person who is *not* liked in a group?
5 Write a little more about the kind of person you described in Box 3	6 What sort of person is *not* like the one you have written about in Box 5? Write as fully as possible.
7 Can you now write a little more about the kind of person who is *not* like the person you have just described in Box 6?	8 Ideas are probably coming to you now. Put down any other ideas you have about the person who is *not* liked by others in group situations.
9 Make final remarks about the kind of person you think is liked by others in a group.	10 Finish by saying something about the kind of person who is not like what you have written in Box 9.

A caution
Students need encouragement when they first try this approach as it seems intimidating at first sight. They should be taken through it carefully.

Follow-up
Students underline key words or phrases. They list them. Discussion with a partner about their ideas follows. The tutor then has a general discussion in which care should be taken to avoid negative criticism or dismissal of students' ideas. When elaboration is required, the

technique of 'reflecting back' as described earlier should be employed.

Leadership, power, innovation, friendship, or any relevant characteristic can be examined. The key to success here lies in the tutor's ability to allow students to examine their ideas afterwards. (This technique can also be used in individual counselling.)

A simpler and more direct approach is shown below. Tutors should point out that no names are to be given on the sheets.

Describe the kind of person you like in a group situation	Describe the kind of person you do *not* like in a group situation

When the students have filled in the question sheet, the tutor initiates discussion in groups of four. After seven minutes, he asks the groups to rank the qualities of liked and disliked individuals, using the 'ladder' approach. Attention should be paid to the rewards coming to us from people we like in group situations.

Other areas of group interaction
Even enthusiastic teachers can take innovations and prevent them from working, because they fail to realise the skill needed, and give insufficient attention to the attitudes of students and the fears of colleagues. Group interaction is an area of threat for many people, therefore stereotypes and prejudice abound. There is real need for caution, since procedures which violate personal space carry a high element of risk. Personal space creates a protective buffer, not only for the body, but for protection of self-respect (Dosey and Meisels, 1969). Like our clothes, it becomes part of us. Students react to such procedures by defensive appraisal, saying, 'What is the point?' Others' feelings of inadequacy are deepened.

Research in this field is relatively meagre, although interesting indications exist. According to Hildreth *et al* (1971), the violent and aggressive have larger areas of personal space than the non-violent. They react to the violation of their personal space sharply. Introverts have larger zones of personal space than do extroverts – Williams (1971) shows their relative vulnerability very clearly. Normative social distances seem to be a product of personality, learning and the setting. Caution is advisable. To use methods which violate personal space is not so much to do harm as invite repudiation and loss of credibility.

Leadership

Leadership – and its correlate, power – are key issues for young adults, yet their concepts of them are naïve. Elementary analysis of the leader-follower relationship shows that followers are not the creatures of a frozen social matrix. Bargaining takes place. One quickly sees that some of the power lies with the followers. Changes of group activity and innovation by the leader posit problems of trust and credibility, as Hollander (1964) suggests in his theory of the accumulation and dissipation of leader credits.

Students occasionally assume unquestioningly that leadership is solely a personality quality, ignoring the nature of the situation in which leadership is exercised. Insufficient attention is given to:

1 The expectation of others.
2 The skills and knowledge demanded by the situation.
3 The style or way in which leadership is exercised by the individual.

One way of introducing the topic is to ask students to discuss and delineate leadership qualities and skills demanded in the following situations.

1 A crisis on an Outward Bound mountain expedition in a blizzard where one member of the party has received severe injuries.
2 A manager has to deal with workers' grievances which could quickly escalate into a strike.
3 An officer with a team of commandos is under fire from the enemy, cut off from his main support group.
4 A youth leader planning, and taking, a party of members for a fortnight's holiday abroad.

Students select three of the four situations. Large circles (10 cms in diameter) are drawn in different colours.

Qualities belonging to the leadership of only one situation are then inserted. Then those found in two of the three. Finally, those common to all three are entered in the appropriate area. (The element of choice in selecting three out of the four seems to add interest.)

Next, the expectations of others and the behaviours or qualities which seem to attract expectations of leadership can be examined. They will include:

1 Physical appearance.
2 Likeability.
3 Verbal fluency.
4 Energy and activity.

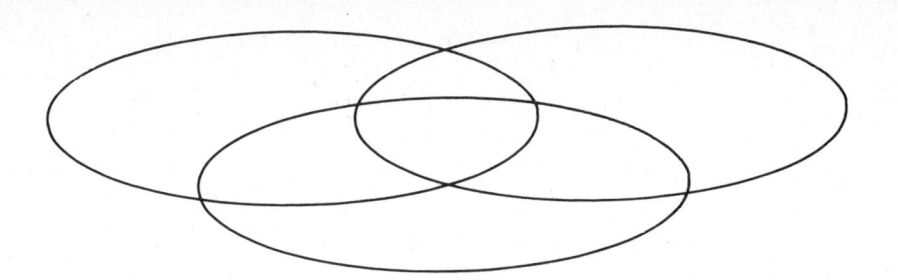

Discussion should cover their feelings about leadership. This includes small-group discussion on the way students think they would behave in particular situations of leadership. The equivalent of the actual/ideal self-discrepancy can be introduced, i.e., the difference between 'the way I would like to behave' and 'the way I think I should behave'. Tutor vigilance is essential to avoid equally unhelpful self-derogation or phantasy. The reality and significance of alleged discrepancies should be pursued without deflation of the student. People can expect too much of themselves, yet they must have an ideal to attain.

Other processes
Evidence from research in behaviour modification, e.g. Thoresen and Mahoney (1974) and Watson and Tharp (1972), indicates that observation of self and others is a necessary part of developing competence. Care has to be taken to respect the vulnerability of this age group, but discussion leads to awareness of forces which inhibit effectiveness and reduce satisfaction. Difficulties do not lie solely in the psyche. They also emanate from the life space of the individual. For the tutor providing guidance the principles are:
1 Observation plus verbalisation aid student self-control.
2 Scanning of possibilities and anticipation of consequences lead to better coping.

Students can be encouraged to examine:
1 *Pairing* This appears when stress or unwelcome features are found in a group. Mutual support and insulation from the pressures give security. The pair may collude to attack vulnerable individuals. Often they develop their own definition of the situation, e.g., 'Making the best of a bad job', or a hidden curriculum of 'Getting through with minimal trouble'.
2 *Opinion leaders* General discussion of leadership can lead to observation of opinion leaders, asking what values they hold and what qualities they possess. This leads students to think about their models. It has proved useful to take cartoons of different

types, e.g., a stolid type apparently oozing respectability and determination, a hearty athletic character, and a 'way-out' individual. Students are asked to predict what they think such characters will have achieved by the age of thirty. They should give reasons for their predictions. Discussion brings out stereotypes and the complexity of the factors involved. If students learn only the fallacious nature of easy judgements the exercise is worthwhile.

Discussion of opinion leaders can raise questions about the kind of person the student would like to emulate. Examination of the successful person follows.

1 What skills have they acquired?
2 What behaviours do they exhibit?
3 What general skills are necessary for success in the current economic climate?

3 *Risks and group behaviours* The phenomenon of the 'risky shift' in group decisions has been explored in depth by Kogan and Wallach (1967), Lamm *et al.* (1971) and McCauley *et al.* (1973). We cannot assume that group forces inevitably increase the level of risk in behaviour, sometimes they induce caution. Students should examine what increases the likelihood of risky behaviour and what reduces it. It seems that a constellation of factors may contribute to a rise in risk: diffusion of responsibility, the effect of familiarity with a situation, successful minor exploits by individuals and 'taking a chance' as a value within the group. The situation is complex and the findings uncertain. Certainly, no single-factor explanation is adequate. Neither can we transfer explanations from one group situation to another validly. Zimbardo's (1969) 'deinviduation' explanation is illuminating. Anonymity and conditions where responsibility cannot be allocated precisely facilitate dangerous and harmful behaviour. If membership of the group is supported by rituals of name and regalia, and reinforced by hostile reactions from others, risks may be discounted. Group counselling uses simple points of departure – allowing the tutor to assess the best strategy for further exploration, e.g.

1 A group of you are out on a Saturday night when you catch sight of a rival group leaving their motorcycles outside a disco. One of you who was beaten up – not badly – by them recently in a quarrel over a girl suggests this is a chance to pay them back for what they did.

What would make you decide to accept or reject his suggestion?

2 Your group of five are at an away soccer match when cans thrown by rival supporters strike you. Violence has occurred on the field, and you feel the rival players got away with it to the

detriment of your own team. The police are preoccupied with incidents at the other side of the stands. You are away from home and not known.

Do you retaliate?

Care is needed. Creation of confrontations in discussion is unprofitable because it polarizes the opinions of young people. Attack alienates them. Crude moralization is a form of collusion, blocking development. Calm explanation of the factors involved and impartial analysis is more likely to succeed. Prudential morality is not to be despised in this area where emotive factors are strong. Casual reinforcement of sensible ideas emerging from group members is advocated. Let us realise that once young adults get caught up in these situations, with overwhelming pressure from peers to avoid loss of face, the thrill of attack takes over.

We can, however, help them examine trigger situations, as described earlier, or cope with the costs and consequences more sensibly. Ways of breaking the pattern of behaviour in a group, or of using humour in the early stages to take out the heat can be considered. Humour, however, can be misconstrued. Keeping face in situations of provocation is worthy of in-depth examination. It is best for students to produce examples of such pressures – this ensures we do not impose our ideas on them. What is threat for us may not be threat for them.

Aggressive behaviour Physical aggression is merely one type of aggression: indirect and psychological forms of aggression are often more worrying to the 16 - 19 year-old. A girl finds it hard to cope with psychological aggression when those mounting a campaign against her get her into a room, standing between her and the door. They make deeply hurtful remarks about her, symbolising her isolation by standing in a loose circle facing inwards. When she protests, they ignore her remarks, tighten the circle, and say something even more diminishing. Psychological aggression thus renders the girl powerless and pushes her into the role of a non-person. Character assassination amongst girls, slights about masculinity in boys, are typical forms with which young adults need help. Sarcasm is the most obvious form, provoking reactions in which a demeaned person resorts to physical aggression for which he is then blamed. I find the old childhood chant is best re-interpreted for this age group as, 'Sticks and stones will hurt my bones, but names are far more harmful!' Helping students take the standpoint of those subjected to psychological aggression is helpful. Discussion of the question, 'Why should people resort to this?' has produced insights.

We should also consider passive forms of aggression. Awareness of their infantile and self-defeating character can only be helpful. Groups of students adopt attitudes which force teachers to nag at them. The nagging they have stimulated is then used to justify their attitudes. Circularity has to be broken by humour. Direct criticism strengthens the responses. I have sometimes begun by saying, 'If I get angry, it's because you made me so, but if you get angry, it's because you are aggressive! Let's look at this.' I may be told that my statement is unfair. We begin to look critically at the falsity of my statement, and go on to examine what is happening between class and teachers. Patronage and the adoption of a superior stance invite rejection and provoke aggression. Counselling has always stressed the 'here and now'. With the 16 - 19 age group we need to apply this principle to the interaction between them and their teachers.

6: Thinking about thinking and learning about learning

Summary points

1. The style of thought and mode of problem-solving is as proper an object of enquiry for this age group as is the content of learning. The focus is therefore on meaningful methods of processing knowledge.
2. Cognitive style or a typical way of thinking which is largely independent of the context or subject should be explored in guidance sessions. Tendencies to close early, refusal to admit further evidence after an initial judgement, over-reliance on the source of a message rather than rational evaluation of content are examples of factors which constrain students' performance and are topics for guidance sessions.
3. Students benefit from examination of the fallacies in judgements, whilst their ideas about causality should be submitted to rigorous scrutiny. When this is linked with the development of sound inferential thinking and the questioning of assumptions, students are more likely to be responsible socially as well as intellectually.
4. Processing information through diagrams and effective reading skills help many young people. Diagrams stimulate the elimination of redundancy, accurate discrimination between the salient and the peripheral, classification and grouping of facts in a meaningful way and detection of relationships.
5. The legacy of learned helplessness and passivity has to be tackled. This should develop into acquisition of mastery techniques and the fostering of originality and the independence of thought.

Why is this necessary?
In *Teaching Study Skills* I argued that pastoral care is an attack on inert and passive forms of learning. If certain processes operate to constrain performance, it is sensible to stimulate awareness of them in students. The 16 - 19 year-old is clear he wants success and good qualifications, but learning is still an amorphous process for many.

Misconceived ideas of the way success is achieved are commonplace, as are over-reliance on memorising, and lack of skill in processing and applying reading and classroom teaching. My practical experience is that this age group is prepared, often fascinated, to take the opportunity to think about their thinking and problem-solving, provided that:

1. the tutor does not monopolise the time telling them how he thinks they ought to think;
2. they are given interesting activities which form the experiential basis for self-examination.

This simple instrument can stimulate a great deal of thought and discussion, although, if given without subsequent discussion and other follow-up activity, it can be sterile.

Attitudes to learning

	Like me	Unlike me
1 I overcome frustrations and difficulty by examining what I do, rather than giving up and say I can't do it.	☐	☐
2 I set myself high standards which I struggle to maintain, even when others say I am working too hard.	☐	☐
3 I get more satisfaction and pleasure from tackling a problem that is difficult to solve than from one which does not 'stretch' me.	☐	☐
4 If I have a choice, I prefer to tackle problems of the type where I have experienced difficulty rather than ones where I know I can succeed.	☐	☐
5 I enjoy working in a group where others are as good as I am, and I have to work to compete with them.	☐	☐
6 Even if I think my answer is incorrect, I will give it, rather than giving an answer only when I know it is right.	☐	☐
7 When I am feeling unwell I still try to complete my assignments rather than put them off.	☐	☐
8 When I play a game (e.g., chess or tennis) I enjoy it most when my opponent is slightly better than I am.	☐	☐

9 I get pleasure from doing a difficult question or essay without help, rather than asking someone for hints about the way to do it. ☐ ☐

10 I am prepared to put my own point of view and support it by reasoned argument and evidence, rather than just repeat what I have read or been told. ☐ ☐

11 Even when someone makes sarcastic remarks about my achievement in a subject I refuse to be put off. ☐ ☐

12 I use criticism as a means of improving my work instead of taking it personally. ☐ ☐

The purpose of this scale

1 It will be obvious that the items are concerned with the learning style that brings success in the sixth form or higher education college. It is easy to endorse the success-orientated box, but not so easy to do it in real life. Learning brings anxiety and self-doubt as we strive to be the best that we can be.

2 It will be helpful if you make some comments on your feelings about three of the items, and then discuss them in more depth. Please write comments in the boxes.

Even when someone makes sarcastic remarks about my achievement in a subject I refuse to be put off.

I enjoy working in a group where the others are as good as I am, and I have to work to compete with them.

I set myself high standards which I struggle to maintain, even when others say I am working too hard.

Subsequent small-group discussion should focus on the ease with which socially desirable answers can be given, which have little relation to what actually happens. I find it helpful to illustrate this by an example from my own behaviour – this certainly focuses attention on the issue. Then the implications of responses to the three items set out in the boxes at the end of the scale can be discussed. In another session the significance of Items 5, 6 and 12 should be gone into. The weighting is towards small-group discussion because the topics arouse either defensiveness or superficially conforming responses. Earlier barren definitions of the classroom situation and defensiveness can be evoked. The competent tutor will, of course, bring matters into the open without being pejorative.

Style of thought

An age of change demands open and adventurous minds. Child-rearing and school experience often develop early closure on problems, passivity and undue reliance upon familiar coping strategies although they are outmoded. The 16 - 19 period may offer the last opportunity for individuals to discard outworn frames of reference and inadequate thought before later pressures restrict them. Recognition of incompetence in problem-solving techniques and self-limiting styles of thought can only increase personal responsibility. Such awareness enhances integrity and maintains the desire for mastery essential to positive mental health even when teaching methods and the attitudes of some teachers discourage initiative and independent thought.

This area of guidance has its limitations: there is no claim that skills will transfer automatically to the student's work. The aim is to increase awareness of strengths and weaknesses which impede attainment of self-set goals. No recipe for thinking or learning is provided because it would not work. Each one of us brings to a learning situation a unique constellation of previous experiences, the products of family attitudes about school, personality factors and peer group pressures, which determines our response. Of no less importance is the need to make concrete situations the basis of much of the work on thought – the weighting will differ with the group.

Group guidance sessions should help students evaluate their beliefs about what brings success in learning. Consideration of the following attributes and their relation to success is the first step:
 – use of intelligence and ability;
 – determination to succeed;
 – concentration;
 – powers of organisation;
 – conscientiousness;
 – enjoyment of learning;
 – questioning mind;
 – sensitivity to praise or blame.

In individual counselling I have found it helpful to encourage students to construct their personal list of what is necessary for success. Then they make a profile assessing where they stand on each attribute. It has also been used with a small group where profiles were compared and the significance of differences evaluated. For some interesting work on sixth form students' constructs used in evaluation of their study the reader should consult Smith (1982).

There is little value in restricted forms of study skills which suggest 'a right way' and which ignore other valid considerations. Defences against learning have to be examined next. Tutors will need to induce greater sensitivity to self-management and responsibility. Students have sometimes learned to reject responsibility for their learning, blaming others for their failures. The ethos developed in the secondary school in earlier years may have reinforced this tendency. Breach of such stereotyped defences has to be achieved by simple activities:

1 Students blame their peer groups or claim they have no time. Guidance sessions can examine the reality of fears of negative labelling by peers of individuals' work. The validity of 'having no time' is questioned. The self-defeating nature of such reactions becomes clear to at least some students.

2 Parents and teachers often become the objects of blame in those motivated to avoid challenge. It is an up-grading of the infant-school child's accusation to his parents, 'Well, I couldn't help it, you made me do it.' Straightforward discussion of such tendencies helps, especially if humour is used to alleviate tensions.

3 Self-management involves discovering the *pattern* of learning which suits the student best. We are aware of rhythms in physiology, but are less aware of them in study. It is useful to ask these questions.

   a What is the best time of day to do certain things?
   Distinguish between the receptive and active, e.g., between assimilation of new ideas or facts and processing or applying them. There is no ideal pattern, only strategies which suit individuals. The risk, e.g., of working better very late in the evening, have to be considered, but the student has to take the responsibility.

   b What is the most effective way to use a block of study time? Is it more productive to work straight through? Is it better to break it down into shorter periods, either changing topics or having a brief rest? If the latter seems more productive, is it best to have a short warm-up period followed by two longer ones, or does more benefit come from a longer initial period followed by two shorter ones?

4 Closely associated with lack of self-management and rejection of responsibility are self-defeating manoeuvres of reality. Tutors should cover:
   a Coping with frustration. Procrastination and pretence of not caring are the equivalent of 'cutting off one's nose to spite one's face'.
   b If avoidance and delay in tackling assignments is a marked feature, do students use nearly as much time and energy in justifying their behaviour as they would in doing the task?
   c Do they gloomily predict failure and, because of this, work without zest and active purpose?
   d Do they transform discontent with their performance into aggression or a 'cocksureness' which not only hides inner insecurity, but which progressively alienates them from the people who offer support?

Guidance is tough-minded in that it faces issues squarely. It is the toughness of compassion, however, which insists that the approach is positive, and that students are shown ways of coping, whilst their positive endeavours are reinforced consistently.

*Further work on cognitive style**
I have used the following materials with a number of large sixth forms. Those taking pre-vocational courses will need the ideas introduced more gradually with sharper structuring by the tutor. I have found, however, that non-traditional sixth-form students benefit from the discussion and activities. In one instance, when working with a sixth form which contained a very high proportion of students from disadvantaged background taking courses other than A-level ones, teachers commented, 'We didn't realise they could do it,' and 'It looks as if we've been babying them and expecting too little. Small-group discussion, in which the groups are composed of students of different ability, seems to produce a productive learning climate from which all benefit. The tutor must, however, modify the materials as he thinks fit.

---

* The activities which follow have been developed from many sources over the last twelve years. I would like to acknowledge my indebtedness to the writers whose work has stimulated them.

Simple cognitive styles: their relevance to your success

Understanding your thinking

1 Success at A-level and in higher education depends on your style of thought and method of problem-solving as much as on hard work and intelligence. Paying attention to them puts you in control of your learning.

2 Sixth-form work requires more than memorising. You have to learn to:
   a assess the evidence for your conclusion;
   b reason deductively;
   c make the skill of appraisal of the strengths and weaknesses of arguments part of your thinking.

   Brief tutor exposition is helpful here.

3 You must get rid of ideas about the right answer or the right way of study. Examine the mature thinker's idea of truth and compare it with the inefficient thinker's definition.

Truth seen as CONDITIONAL PROPOSITIONAL RELATIVE	Truth seen as FIXED AND FINAL ABSOLUTE REVELATORY

4 Discuss this point:
   Scientific advance involves an unending process of conjecture, exploration, testing, followed by confirmation or refutation. The history of science shows that many discarded theories aided progress despite their eventual rejection.

The idea of cognitive style

1 As we pass through childhood and adolescence we adopt habitual ways of tackling problems and learning tasks. We take them for granted; indeed, we are unaware of them. In late adolescence they crystallise into a cognitive style.

> *What is cognitive style?*
> It is:
> a A way of thinking which is independent of specific topics or subjects.
> b A characteristic way of operating which can be detected in the way people see things, relate to other people and evaluate the nature of evidence.
> c The way in which we process information and give meaning to what we learn.

Are you an authoritarian thinker?

1 Being an authoritarian thinker has little to do with authority figures. 'Authoritarian' describes a way of seeing the world and a style of thinking.

2 Here are the main characteristics of the authoritarian thinkers

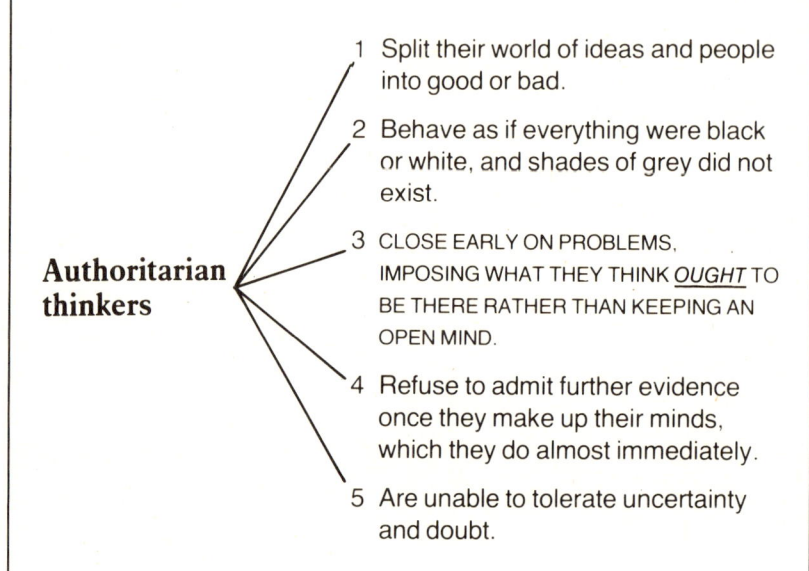

Authoritarian thinkers

1 Split their world of ideas and people into good or bad.

2 Behave as if everything were black or white, and shades of grey did not exist.

3 CLOSE EARLY ON PROBLEMS, IMPOSING WHAT THEY THINK <u>OUGHT</u> TO BE THERE RATHER THAN KEEPING AN OPEN MIND.

4 Refuse to admit further evidence once they make up their minds, which they do almost immediately.

5 Are unable to tolerate uncertainty and doubt.

3 Examine the five points given above and discuss with a partner.
   a How they might affect capacity to learn new material.
   b The impact on problem-solving.
   Then make comments below.

4 Two more facts about authoritarian thinkers:
   a They see the world as threatening and easily feel that 'things are being done to them.'
   b They dislike what is unfamiliar or new and tend to deride it.
   What does this add to your knowledge of this style of thinking? Discuss the authoritarian thinker's ability to use and to apply what he is taught.

The dogmatist

1 His characteristics are:

| a Relying on authority for his ideas. | b Having strong belief systems about what is true and what is false. He keeps them quite separate. | c Rarely, if ever, questioning his beliefs. |

2 What does this do to his thinking?

   a Research suggests that he tends to judge statements more on *where they come from* than on the content. He relies on the source to give information credibility, i.e., *who* says it is more important that *what* is said.

   b He can explore a problem quite well, but he finds it difficult to be original or creative because his belief systems are so strong. His dogmatism makes it difficult for him to replace old beliefs and ideas by new ones.

   c Discuss in a small group of three or four people what areas of thought and which topics are susceptible to dogmatism. Write your conclusions below, justifying them.

   d The dogmatist finds it difficult to look at things from a different viewpoint. Like the authoritarian thinker, he has a closed mind, and sees only one way of looking at things. Examine your conclusions above critically, and see if you can construct a counter-argument. Discuss it first. Put your counter-argument below.

   e Here is a dogmatic statement:

   > There are two kinds of people in this world: those who are for the truth and those who are against the truth.

   Why is it dogmatic? Discuss and give reasons.

Levelling and sharpening

1 Many workers have shown that, when we listen to people and then report what they have said, we tend to simplify and focus only on what is significant to us. In the old game of 'Whispers' the message whispered along the row of players is often totally changed by the time the last one gets it. In rumour and crisis situations facts are distorted. Some facts are given more importance and assume salience, while others are reduced in importance or ignored. But we all tend to be either sharpeners or levellers.

> **Some of us tend to see everything as of equal importance: others focus on a few points that they believe to be of importance**

2 Try to answer these questions. Do not consult your friends.
   a When I meet a problem, do I scan it thoroughly or do I tend to concentrate almost immediately on a few points that seem important?
   b What makes me decide what is significant?

3 You probably found it hard to answer these questions. The following problem may help you learn about the way you scan and select.
   a You are on a sinking yacht in the South Seas. All your companions have been lost in the storm. You can get to an uninhabited island, but the small boat will allow you to take only ten of the items listed below. Which ones would you choose? It will be some weeks, possibly months, before you are rescued.

   1 spade
   2 case of tinned meat
   3 wireless receiver – battery operated
   4 matches – 1 dozen boxes
   11 3 heavy jerseys
   12 blankets
   13 drill – hand type
   14 plastic sheeting
   15 box of screws and nails

5 first-aid kit
6 axe – heavy
7 coil of rope – 60 ft. length
8 compass
9 clock – spring type
10 large water container

16 case of tinned fruit
17 kettle and cups
18 flares and smoke bombs
19 folding bed
20 Wellington boots

Put your ten articles below:

b Now spell out the principles underlying your choice and relate them to the need to survive. Did you scan the situation and think of difficulties which might occur in a few weeks? Did some items seem to assume immediate importance? If so, why?

c Now complete the following sentences:

   i   When I begin to assess a problem ....
       ....

   ii When in doubt ....
       ....

   iii Selecting key issues ....
       ....

   iv My strategy for solving a problem ....
       ....

   v   At the end of the problem I realise ....
       ....

d Describe what you believe to be the way you assess and tackle a problem in the subject you enjoy most.

4 The following exercise may make you aware of the way you focus on key elements in a problem situation.

You are in charge of rescue operations in a small town which has been devasted by a cyclone. Bridges, roads and rail links have been destroyed. It is therefore cut off from major help for another 48 hours. Electricity and gas are not available. Telephone communication is impossible within the area. Sewage has contaminated the water supply. The hospital is only just coping with the injured. To add to the general misery, sporadic outbursts of looting are occurring.

Describe the way you would tackle the problem.

Now discuss with three or four friends:

a The ways in which you all made your initial decisions.
b Which aspects were given immediate priority and why.
c Which problems in such a situation you felt could be left and why this was so.
d Criticise your approach constructively.

5 *The implications of levelling and sharpening*
If the problem solver focuses immediately on certain features as the significant ones, ignoring others, he may find that unanticipated consequences prevent him from dealing with these others later on. To seize immediately on one or two aspects without scanning carefully may distort the problem by sharpening or giving an undeserved importance to certain items.

It is a form of making up your mind too easily, and then refusing to admit further evidence because you don't see that it will help the solution. In other words, it is a form of early closure similar to that found in the authoritarian thinker.

Scanning is essential, but at some point we have to make a decision about what is important. This sharpens or gives shape to the way we try to solve the problem. We should train ourselves to ask, 'Why is this important?' The thinker who sees everything as equally important is likely to become confused and fail.

The message: it pays to understand your problem-solving style

These exercises are not the equivalent of a work sheet which demands little participation from the teacher. Tutors should follow small-group discussion with general discussion, allowing issues to emerge. Small-group discussion or partner work can follow to explore them. The exercises are a point of departure. Inability to tolerate ambiguity and uncertainty, which is associated with anxiety and leads to early closure or impulsive reaction, can be the initial topic. Tutors can then move to critical examination by students of their approach to problems and their use of evidence. The activities which follow have captured the interest of students, although their efficacy depends on the post-activity discussion.

Understanding your approach to problem-solving

Introduction
These simple exercises are intended to help you examine your style of problem-solving. As a young adult seeking success in life you have to analyse the way you solve problems and think about your thinking.

Problem 1
1. Imagine that you are a civil engineer who is making a decision about the best place to build a heavy-duty bridge across a major river. What considerations would be in your mind?
2. Now rank them in order of importance below, and *justify* your ranking.
3. Discuss with a friend how you decide what is important in a problem. Have you thought about this before?

Problem 2
You are on holiday with two other friends and staying at a holiday village. Lots of other young people are there, and they get a bit boisterous at times, raiding one another's chalets. But there are also frequent burglaries in the area. You return to the chalet after a day out – it is nearly midnight. When you enter the chalet you find everything in chaos. Drawers have been emptied, and it looks frightful. You have to decide very quickly whether to inform the police. Access has been through a window you carelessly left open, so the mode of entry gives no clue as to whether it is the work of your friends or not. If it is your friends you do not wish to bring in the police. What evidence will you look for? Put your conclusions below:

Now assess how valid this evidence is likely to be. Examine it critically.

Problem 3
1 Crack this code. The code is consistent throughout the list:

Word	Code form
MARKED	NAZYICPWVEWU
ANT	ZBMZGD
WILD	DARYOCWW
PROPOSAL	KAIYLCKWLEHUZGOS
FLATTER	UBOZZDGXGFVVIH
LARGE	OBZZIDTXVF

Then decipher:

    ZBTZVDMXGF   HALYFCKW

2 What have you learned about assumptions? Give your answer below:

3 What strategies do you have for tackling this type of task, e.g. look for similarities; eliminate possibilities? Outline your approach here; then discuss its efficiency with your partner.

Problem 4
1 *Examine these statements critically, assessing their truth. Discuss them for ten to fifteen minutes in a group of four.*
   a Familiarity breeds contempt
   b Any intelligent person knows that God exists.
1 Now take 'Familiarity breeds contempt'. Ask about the evidence which supports or contradicts the statement. What is distasteful about a statement presented in this way? Make comments below:

3 Examine the implications of 'Any intelligent person knows that God exists'. Look carefully at the significance of 'Any' and 'intelligent'. What is the weakness of such an argument? Why do statements of this type persuade people of their truth? Comment below, please.

Post-activity discussion centres on:
— Feelings about mathematical problems or problems that look as if they were mathematical. Do students not attempt to solve them because the problems seem intimidating? Do they predict they won't be able to do them?
— Do they tackle the problem as set, or do they tend to alter it by leaving out essential conditions?
— Do they keep persevering with an approach, even if it yields no results?
— Have they learned to check apparent solutions carefully?

More work on your method of problem-solving

The purpose of this activity
1 Do not expect too much! There is no way of teaching the skills of problem-solving which will automatically transfer to your subjects. But understanding your usual way of approaching problems and their consequences can be helpful. Talking with friends about the way you learn can put you more in charge of your learning.
2 Now try the 'square problem'.

Number the remaining squares, *without repeating numbers,* so that each *row, column* and *diagonal add up to 15*.
You must keep all the conditions.

If you have not solved it in 5 minutes a hint will be given to you. When you have finished discuss the following:
   a Do I react well or badly to numerical problems? If badly, what do I expect to occur?

b How do I react to the problem? Did I see it as having boundaries within which I can take various paths, e.g., in the square problem did I begin by filling in one line first? If so, why did I choose this line?

3 Next, work on Luchin's water-jug problems. You have to get a certain quantity of water. You have three jugs, all of which are empty. You can fill them, empty them, and pour water from one jug to another.

Problem	Capacity of Jug A	Capacity of Jug B	Capacity of Jug C	Amount of water required
	quarts	quarts	quarts	quarts
1	5	40	18	28
2	21	127	3	100

You have a number of strategies:

FILL   a If one jug is empty and the capacity of the jug is greater than the desired amount, fill the jug.

ADD   b If one jug's capacity is greater than the desired amount and a second jug's capacity is less than the desired amount, fill the second jug and pour the water into the first jug.

SUBTRACT   c If one jug contains more than the desired amount and the capacity of the second jug is less than the contents of the first jug, empty the second jug and pour and the first jug into it.

Problem	Capacity of Jug A	Capacity of Jug B	Capacity of Jug C	Desired Quantity
1	14	163	25	99
2	18	43	10	5
3	9	42	6	21
4	20	59	4	31
5	23	49	3	20
6	15	39	3	18
7	28	76	3	25
8	18	48	4	22

Did you have difficulty with any particular problem? Discuss the reasons for this.

A simple explanation will be given to you of what is called 'set'. Discuss its relevance to your problem-solving.

4 *Devising a plan for problem-solving*
It will be useful if you draw up a plan for problem-solving that suits you. Some hints are given below.

Step 1   Understanding the problems
Ask:
  i   What are the conditions of the problem?
  ii What is the key task to be done?
  iii Does the set of instructions contain clues about the solution?

Step 2   Planning an attack
Ask:
  i   Have I met this type of problem before?
  ii What do I really know that will be useful?
  iii What 'tools' do I have for solving this problem?
  iv Now inspect again all the vital statements made in the problem.
  v   Ensure that you have not left out anything vital.

Step 3
  i   Start work on problem.
  ii When you have finished, check each step.
  iii Finally, evaluate your method. Ask yourself if there was a quicker and better way which you can now see.

Some considerations
1 The influence of *set* can be helpful. Set is the condition in which you have strong expectations about the way the problem *ought* to be solved. This leads to a 'blind' attack on the problem. When one is dealing with a series of problems, there may be a change in the conditions or data which make inappropriate what has previously been a successful method of solution. But the set which has been established makes us press on blindly.
2 *Assumptions* are closely related to, but are not identical with, *set*. Did you, in the squares puzzle, assume that the entries in each cell had to be restricted to whole numbers? You can see that assumptions act as mental 'corsets' which restrict our thought.
3 Those who tend to be anxious are easily conditioned to expect failure or difficulty. Anxiety itself, if strong, acts to reduce powers of discrimination and selection. Therefore the student who reacts to problem-solving situations with excessive anxiety cannot select what is relevant, rendering his attempts abortive. The tendency is then to predict failure, and to opt out.

Summary points
1 Train yourself to scan the problem, looking at the implications.
2 Learn to think in terms of strategies rather than *the* right way.

3. Look for similarities and differences between the problem and others you have met in the past.
4. Watch that you:
   - observe the conditions of the problem rather than impose your own meaning;
   - check what you have done. It is only too easy to delude yourself that you have reached a solution.
5. Above all, talk about your strategies. This puts them under your control, and allows you to extend them.

Solution to Square Problem
You do not necessarily have to rely on whole numbers.

1.5	8	5.5
9	5	1
4.5	2	8.5

The Use of Diagrams
This was dealt with in *Teaching Study Skills*, but there is need for a little more work specifically aimed at the 16 - 19 age group. A number of students – not necessarily following the sciences – possess well developed visual and spatial ability relative to their verbal skill. Diagrams help them process material. This simple diagram, taken from page 48 of *Teaching Study Skills*, illustrates the fundamental merits of diagrams:

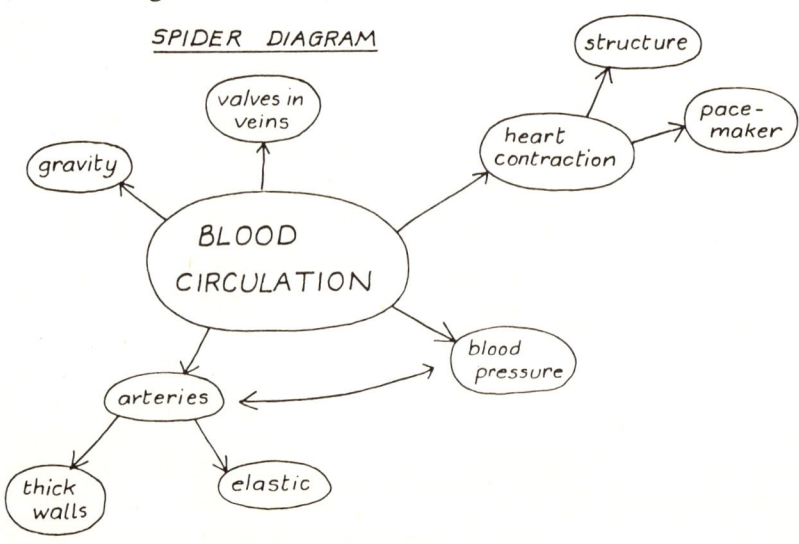

SPIDER DIAGRAM

- BLOOD CIRCULATION
  - valves in veins
  - gravity
  - heart contraction
    - structure
    - pace-maker
  - blood pressure
  - arteries
    - thick walls
    - elastic

1 Redundancy is eliminated.
2 Distinction between what is peripheral and what is salient is represented spatially, i.e., the salient is near the centre.
3 Classification or grouping of related elements is clearly shown.
4 Relationships are shown. There is indication of the direction, e.g., unidirectional → or reciprocal ⟷

Diagrams allow the learner to process information in a way meaningful to him or her. Construction of a diagram means undertaking a cognitive search and selection of elements. Evaluation of their importance is also involved. Strength of relationships can be indicated by the thickness of arrows or the connecting links. Shapes and patterns allow complex material to be apprehended, but more important is the fact that to diagram learning material allows its significance to be retained. At their best, diagrams are more than a cognitive mapping process, for inferences are built in during their construction. Students therefore become more aware of the implications of the subject matter.

Not all students can use diagrams. Although there should be no pressure, the opportunity for experiment should be provided. I recall with pleasure a sixth-form student, whose initial response was one of distaste and belief that he could not use diagrams, giving a brilliant exposition two years later of the value of the technique at a sixth-form induction course. His skill at using diagrams was far beyond my own, despite the unpromising start he had made. He had developed a number of different types of diagram to fit his subjects – a salutary reminder that there is no one right type of diagram. Students' preferences and the structure of the topic provide the guides. The diagrams on p. 156 and p. 157 illustrate how much information can be incorporated.

Structuring reading
Methods of improving reading such as SQ3R are described in earlier work. Tutors can refer to them, but it is vital to remember that passive approaches to reading are associated with over-reliance on learning by heart and lack of processing and application. This is self-defeating, anyway, because blind reading without selection of the salient leaves one with little to remember. A session based on the following provides an introduction to the topic.

Biology notes – detailed web diagram

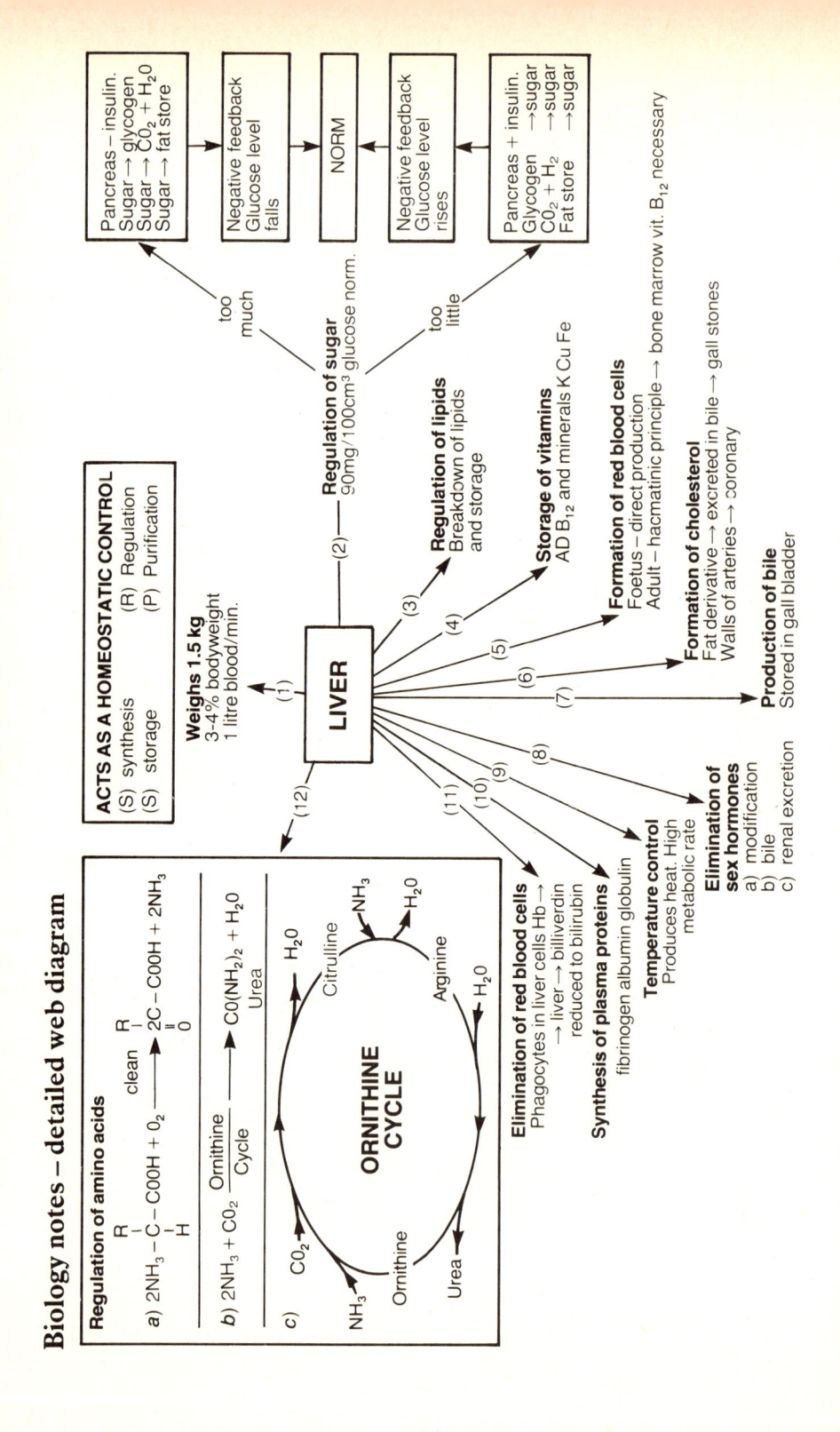

ACTS AS A HOMEOSTATIC CONTROL

(S) synthesis (R) Regulation
(S) storage (P) Purification

LIVER

Weighs 1.5 kg
3–4% bodyweight
1 litre blood/min.

(1)

(2) **Regulation of sugar**
90mg/100cm³ glucose norm.

too much →
- Pancreas – insulin.
- Sugar → glycogen
- Sugar → $CO_2 + H_2O$
- Sugar → fat store

→ Negative feedback Glucose level falls → **NORM** ← Negative feedback Glucose level rises ←

too little →
- Pancreas + insulin.
- Glycogen → sugar
- $CO_2 + H_2$ → sugar
- Fat store → sugar

(3) **Regulation of lipids**
Breakdown of lipids and storage

(4) **Storage of vitamins**
AD B_{12} and minerals K Cu Fe

(5) **Formation of red blood cells**
Foetus – direct production
Adult – hacmatinic principle → bone marrow vit. B_{12} necessary

(6) **Formation of cholesterol**
Fat derivative → excreted in bile → gall stones
Walls of arteries → coronary

(7) **Production of bile**
Stored in gall bladder

(8) **Elimination of sex hormones**
a) modification
b) bile
c) renal excretion

(9) **Temperature control**
Produces heat. High metabolic rate

(10) **Synthesis of plasma proteins**
fibrinogen albumin globulin

(11) **Elimination of red blood cells**
Phagocytes in liver cells Hb → → liver → billiverdin reduced to bilirubin

(12) **Regulation of amino acids**

a) $2NH_3 - \overset{R}{\underset{H}{C}} - COOH + O_2 \xrightarrow{clean} 2C - COOH + 2NH_3$
                                      $\parallel$
                                      O

b) $2NH_3 + CO_2 \xrightarrow{\text{Ornithine Cycle}} CO(NH_2)_2 + H_2O$
   Urea

c) **ORNITHINE CYCLE**

Ornithine → (+CO_2, +NH_3) → Citrulline → (+NH_3, −H_2O) → Arginine → (+H_2O, −Urea) → Ornithine

History notes – flow diagram

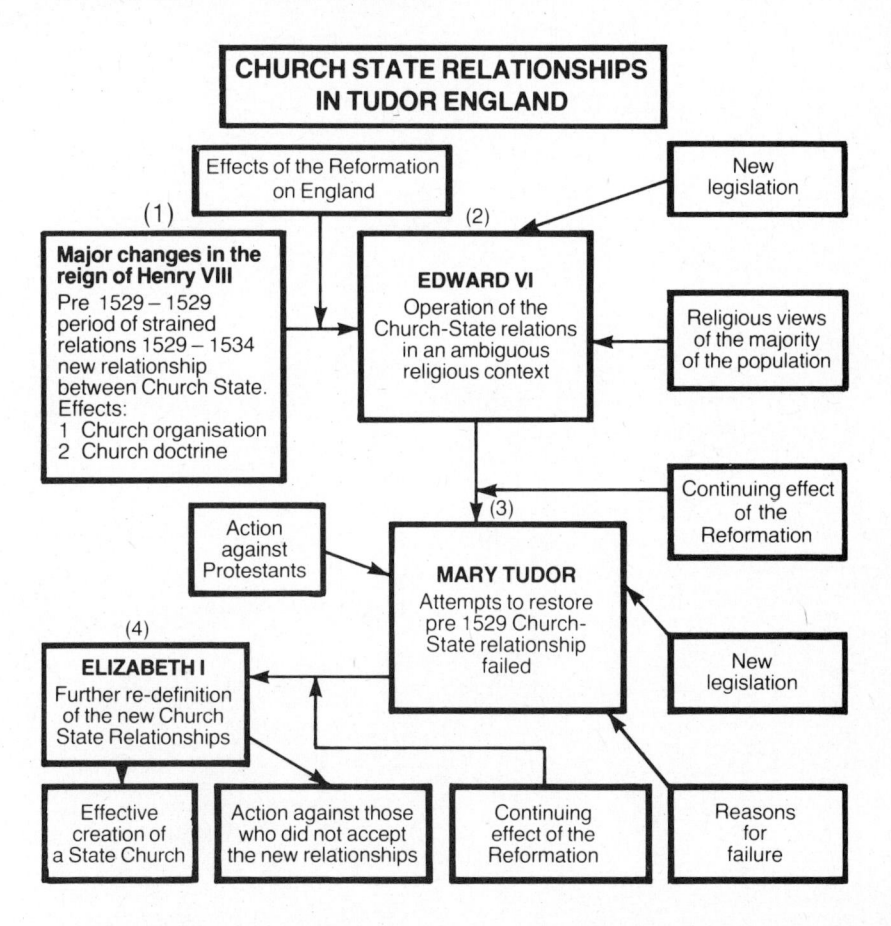

CHURCH STATE RELATIONSHIPS IN TUDOR ENGLAND

Effects of the Reformation on England

(1) **Major changes in the reign of Henry VIII**
Pre 1529 – 1529 period of strained relations 1529 – 1534 new relationship between Church State.
Effects:
1 Church organisation
2 Church doctrine

(2) **EDWARD VI** Operation of the Church-State relations in an ambiguous religious context
- New legislation
- Religious views of the majority of the population

(3) **MARY TUDOR** Attempts to restore pre 1529 Church-State relationship failed
- Action against Protestants
- Continuing effect of the Reformation
- New legislation

(4) **ELIZABETH I** Further re-definition of the new Church State Relationships
- Effective creation of a State Church
- Action against those who did not accept the new relationships
- Continuing effect of the Reformation
- Reasons for failure

Structuring your reading

Basic Points

1 'I'm working two to three hours every evening but I'm not getting anywhere.' Behind this complaint sometimes heard in the second year of the sixth form may lie ineffective reading. To read blindly is to waste time.

2 Students who read through a text or assignment conscientiously still may not be able to recall much of what they have read.

Ask yourself if you have acquired the following skills:
   a Orientating yourself purposefully by getting a clear outline of what the book or chapter contains. (This is the equivalent of consulting a map before you begin a journey into unfamiliar terrain.)

    b Constructing a list of questions that you want to answer.
    c Selecting the key points and searching for clues of importance and significance as you read.
    d Breaking a chapter down into sections once you have got a clear impression of the total task. You then test your recall of that section before going further.
    e Processing the information by constructing a diagram or making a summary using your own words, but making the intention and purpose of the author clear.

Using a flow chart in reading
1. A flow chart can be used as a means of recall. You can arrange what you have learned from the set reading as a flow chart. This will give you a summary which emphasises the sequence or order of the new material.
2. Try to experiment. Take a lesson which was both important and enjoyable. Arrange the key points as a flow chart. You will see the structure of the lesson clearly.

A re-cap on structuring reading
1. Two important aspects forgotten by many people:
    a Constructing a list of questions after you have scanned the chapter.
    b Testing yourself at intervals, and asking not only, 'What did I forget?', but 'Why did I forget it?'

Check your approach to reading against this flow chart
A flow chart is simply a series of boxes, each of which represents a step or activity in the task of reading efficiently. The arrows linking the boxes show the 'flow' or sequence of activities. Arrows at the side of the box lead to other instructions. You will find it useful to apply this approach for three weeks. It is very probable that you will be pleased with the results.

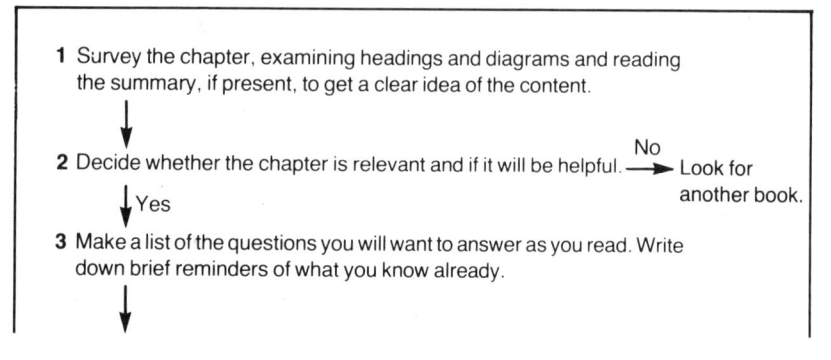

---

1 Survey the chapter, examining headings and diagrams and reading the summary, if present, to get a clear idea of the content.

↓

2 Decide whether the chapter is relevant and if it will be helpful. —No→ Look for another book.

↓ Yes

3 Make a list of the questions you will want to answer as you read. Write down brief reminders of what you know already.

↓

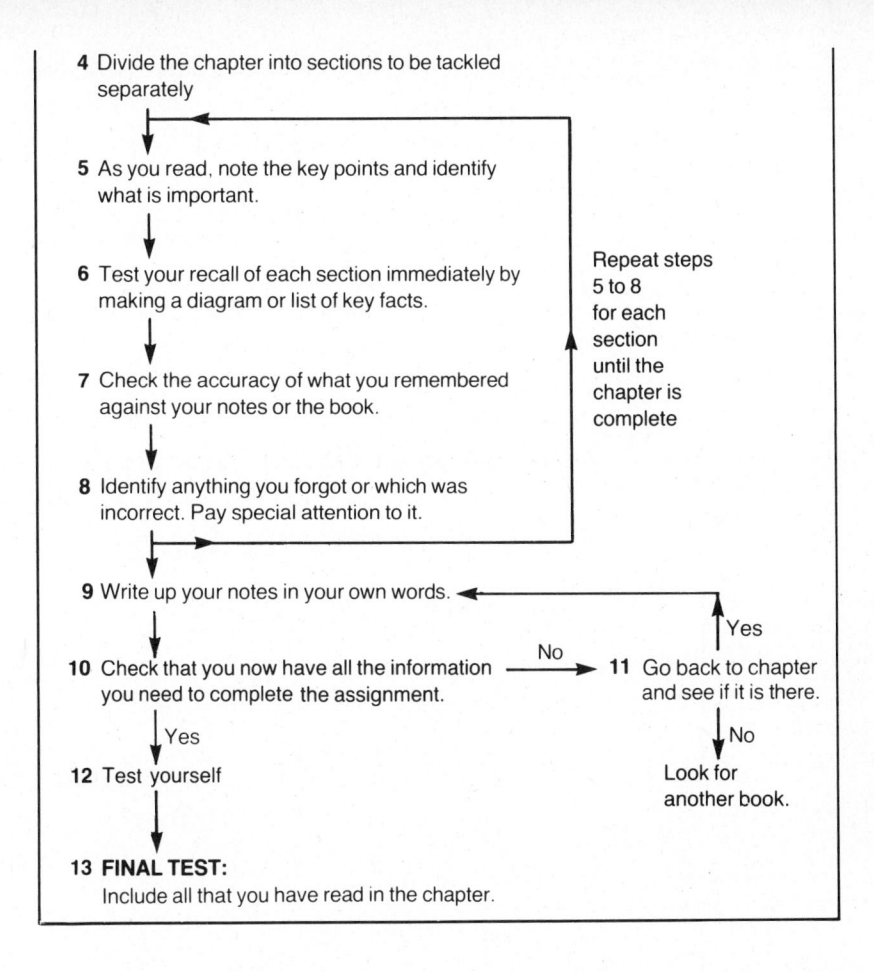

```
4  Divide the chapter into sections to be tackled
   separately
            ↓
5  As you read, note the key points and identify
   what is important.
            ↓
6  Test your recall of each section immediately by     Repeat steps
   making a diagram or list of key facts.              5 to 8
            ↓                                          for each
                                                       section
7  Check the accuracy of what you remembered           until the
   against your notes or the book.                     chapter is
            ↓                                          complete
8  Identify anything you forgot or which was
   incorrect. Pay special attention to it.
            ↓
9  Write up your notes in your own words.  ←──────────────────┐
            ↓                                                 │ Yes
                                      No                      │
10 Check that you now have all the information ──→ 11 Go back to chapter
   you need to complete the assignment.              and see if it is there.
         ↓ Yes                                            ↓ No
12 Test yourself                                       Look for
         ↓                                             another book.
13 FINAL TEST:
   Include all that you have read in the chapter.
```

2 An intimidating assignment is tackled more positively if you split it into sections.

Passivity and Helplessness

Dweck and Licht (1980) suggest it is important to ask which intellectual pursuits are most likely to be hampered by inability to cope with failure, and which are the least likely. This leads us to consider when students feel helpless and incapable of changing a situation of failure or frustration. If the sense of helplessness in learning is strong, individual counselling will be necessary. Tutors will need to apply the behavioural principles of graduation and reinforcement outlined in Chapter 2. One may have to deal with an obstinate tendency in those who have learned to be helpless to attribute any success experienced to luck and not to ability, so that failures are interpreted as a reflection of their true ability. Such students have a well developed capacity for making the tutor feel helpless.

Mathematics and the sciences seem to present the greatest difficulties for those with tendencies towards helplessness. Remember that helplessness implies the student feels that his or her efforts will make no difference to the outcome. Blind encouragement or reassurance will not work. The mathematics teachers must be involved in the guidance. Despite the concern for equality of opportunity emerging in recent years, girls still seem vulnerable to feelings of inadequacy in the sciences. I have met many girls taking A-level chemistry and physics who have experienced problems. Not all stem from internal feelings of helplessness; some girls feel the problems arise from the fact that boys, and occasionally male teachers, do not take them seriously and there is evidence to support this feeling. Perhaps girls are conditioned to be more sensitive to their failures than their successes in evaluating their future success. When under stress, this feeling creates debilitating anxiety.

Let me make it clear that learned helplessness is found in boys too, and has equally detrimental effects on their learning. General guidance sessions which look at the tendency to compare oneself negatively with others, alerting students to the way self-fulfilling prophecies can be created, and which uses the 'one step at a time' approach can alleviate, if not remove, the tendency.

Other aspects of learning and problem solving

1 *Use of evidence*

Students confuse opinion with critical thought. Opinion unbacked by rational argument or evidence is of little academic worth. They tend to assume that the teacher's rejection of opinion indicates inability to tolerate a different viewpoint, or they see it as personal devaluation. Criticism is not seen as an opportunity for intellectual growth or strengthening one's position by examining weaknesses honestly and undertaking realistic modification.

Guidance should help students to look at the validity of the conclusions they draw in argument or academic work. Is there sufficient evidence to support their position? The crude exclusive categorisation of true or false has to be replaced by a wider and more tentative series of judgement. Note, however, this is not about the nature of truth as such, but about the degree of confidence one has in one's conclusions. Probably true, probably false, or insufficient data are categories which give greater malleability to judgements.

The basic skill to be developed is that of appraisal which lacks the one-sidedness often contained in alleged critical thought.

Gradually, students will appreciate the fact that our perception of truth is limited and liable to shaping by many factors. Cultural elements, which include not only, in Mannheimian terms, one's position in a social structure, but the global spirit of the time, partially determine what is salient – perhaps even what is perceived. Personality factors enter, and students find it helpful to discuss the the old Helmholtzian proposition that behaviour is a function of our assumptions. As the individual assumes, so he perceives. Equally, Oppenheim (1966) points out that behaviour is a function of environment not solely as it is, but as it is perceived. Hence, there can be many views of the same event. Discussion of these matters can break into rigidities and produce a healthy respect for other viewpoints, when it occurs within a climate of acceptance and respect. Without this, young people can retreat to the original position, holding it more tenaciously than before.

The above can be linked to the need to encourage students to think hypothetically. Although, as suggested, a proper regard for the evidence is essential, it should be paralleled by encouragement to think also in terms of possibilities. Confusion of the empirical and hypothetical is a danger to which students should be alerted. Diagrams, models and discussion of causality help. Students sometimes fail to see that occurrence together or association does not necessarily allow us to impute a causal relation – like the man from Mars who, on the evidence of observation, decided that fire engines cause fires. Ideas of causality, and realistic flexibility in their application, contribute much to the success or failure of us all.

2 *Constructive questioning*
Appraisal of strengths and weaknesses is sounder than over-reliance on criticism. The latter can become destructive or may reflect a need to gain identity by opposition which has been extended to the intellectual field. In Chapter 4 it was pointed out that students are unable to ask meaningful questions in interviews. In stimulating thinking about thinking we should help the student question the questions. Society needs at all levels people who can ask if the problem as defined is the real problem. Is the formulation of the problem valid? Those who work in managerial positions – including those within schools and colleges – are well aware that system trouble generates defensive obstacles which obscure the real problem. Tutors, through these subjects, can give something of inestimable value to students, the orientation and ability to raise and detect problems.

3 *Creativity*

There is no space to analyse this concept in depth. Yet it will become more important to foster creativity in a largely unpredictable future. As a teacher, I still find the views of Lowenfeld (1957) and Read (1958) compelling. We may deny imagination and undervalue creative subjects in a dreary emphasis on survival skills. Imagination is not the prerogative of the artist, it extends to every field of human endeavour. The scientist without imagination is limited, perhaps a menace. The creative scientist is aware – often uncomfortably so – of the subjectivity of his speculations.

Creativity, from my viewpoint, is not making something out of nothing, but giving structure where none existed or providing an alternative to what exists. It is the ability to see relationships where none were seen, the capacity to discard assumptions temporarily and view problems from a different standpoint.

Tutors can do something to help students acquire these abilities, helping them escape the rigidity of conventional response. This remark is not an attack on the acquisition of knowledge, for it is impossible to be creative in any significant way without a well stocked mind. But one's stock of ideas and knowledge may be inert.

a Students can be encouraged to use brain-storming techniques as a prelude to tackling a problem. Students produce ideas which are written down without comment or criticism. They are asked not to evaluate their own ideas as irrelevant or useless, but to share them. Then the group discusses the potentialities of the ideas collected.

b Small groups work for 15 - 20 minutes developing an 'ideas bank' about what can be included in an essay or assignment, thus extending their frames of reference.

c The ideas bank can be extended to ways of tackling a learning task. Tutors who welcome initiative and independence will find it profitable to give students the opportunity to verbalise their strategies for tackling it. This will include the type of question put forward in Marland (Ed.) (1981), e.g., 'What information do I need? Where do I go for it? How do I record it? What is the best way of presenting the assignment?' I advocate students working together to question assumptions and share ideas about what works in that type of task. As a result, a strategy is produced which can be evaluated by them rather than solely by the teacher. Tutors will find it useful to get feedback from students about their progress after 20 minutes' work on the task. This allows help to be offered and the sense of purpose to be sharpened. (Obviously this is done only occasionally.) Evaluation of the success of the strategy can be through small groups, followed by a class discussion. Check lists or profiles can be used by students as part of formative evaluation. Constructive self and peer evaluation becomes an integral element of assessment.

d   Opportunity must be given for exploration of beliefs about why young people of their age fail or succeed as learners. All too often, the concept of oneself as a learner is ignored.

e   If creativity and initiative is to be achieved, we should share with students our beliefs about the nature and objectives of education. This is not an abrogation of responsibility, but an ethical act of justification. Negotiation has been stressed throughout this book. We may well find ourselves enriched as professionals if we take it seriously.

Epilogue

We should accept that no ideal guidance programme exists or is likely to exist. Attempts to impose programmes on this age group are doomed to failure because they create indifference and alienate tutors from students.

In constructing the modules of guidance, materials will be drawn from many sources and adapted to meet the needs of students and tutors in a specific institution. Construction of modules is best based on Davies's (1976) idea of piecemeal objectives, which implies a series of gradual approximations through which we become aware of what will work. A means/end dialogue is initiated in which we ask what worked and why, what failed and why. Failure is not passively accepted, but becomes the object of enquiry. What is essential is the process of negotiation with students and their involvement in the selection and construction of materials. Teacher/lecturer confidence is crucial. Resistance or lack of caring in the student often stems from teachers' ignorance about guidance and the way it contributes to the achievement of educational objectives. Colleagues should be helped to see that a system of guidance has to be developed over four to six years, and that development will reflect the professional skills of staff. They may anticipate having to battle with students to get them to accept guidance, instead of seeing that pupils can be involved as participants in designing and operating a guidance module. King *et al.* (1974) found that 16 - 19 year-olds strongly desired more guidance and counselling. I have had first-hand experience of self-help groups and of peer counselling schemes, such as Williams (1973) described.

Doherty (1981) illuminates evaluation. Meaning gradually emerges as monitoring proceeds. Even those engaged in guidance may not at first recognise the forces at play. For those who monitor guidance, 'truth' certainly is propositional and all reality necessarily multiple. The reality of guidance is different for student, tutor and senior management. Similarly, we must beware the fallacy of talking about *the* school or *the* college. Like the curate's egg, educational institutions are good, bad or indifferent in parts.

Monitoring often focuses sharply on the tutor's role. It is necessary to distinguish systematically between:
- *prescribed role* as laid down in job descriptions and official documents;
- *interpreted role* which stems from the holder's beliefs and characteristics;
- *expected role* which is a product of the beliefs and expectations of others and often associated with contradictions and conflict;
- *performed role*.

Monitoring should encourage what Turner (1970) has described as a dynamic process of role-taking and role-making, allowing adjustment to current conditions and needs, but also allowing tutors to exercise professional autonomy. There must be honest communication and sensitivity to trends if tutor work is not to become a token activity.

Next, the group of tutors could look at the balance of task orientation and relationship orientation, avoiding the assumption that an ideal 'mix' exists independently of the institutional context. Mythologies are strong in guidance – people behave as if an ideal performance or state of affairs exists from which all others are deviant. Critical incidents, which have to be resolved for efficiency, should be identified and watched carefully. Blocks and hazards, e.g., insufficient time or conflict between roles must be made visible and debated. We cannot delude ourselves that all conflict can be eliminated: indeed, the desirability of this, if it could be achieved, is debatable. Consensus will never be achieved, and realistic clashes of interest cannot be talked out of existence. Evaluators have to ask, 'What is negotiable, and what cannot be modified?' Teachers' beliefs about broader issues – the nature of ability, student motivation, what can be achieved and how – have to be taken into account.

Patterns of relationships and approaches to teaching which we disapproved of or find difficult to understand may be strategies for survival first learned in the probationary year. Failure to appreciate this prevents us from adjusting demands to what is tolerable for the individual. If we cannot take the standpoint of such colleagues, the result will be an increase in their resistance to change.

I end with a simple outline I used recently in working with a group. Ideally, such a framework should be devised by tutors and students. Self-created frameworks for evaluation are more useful than any others.

1 INPUT TO GUIDANCE SUB-SYSTEM

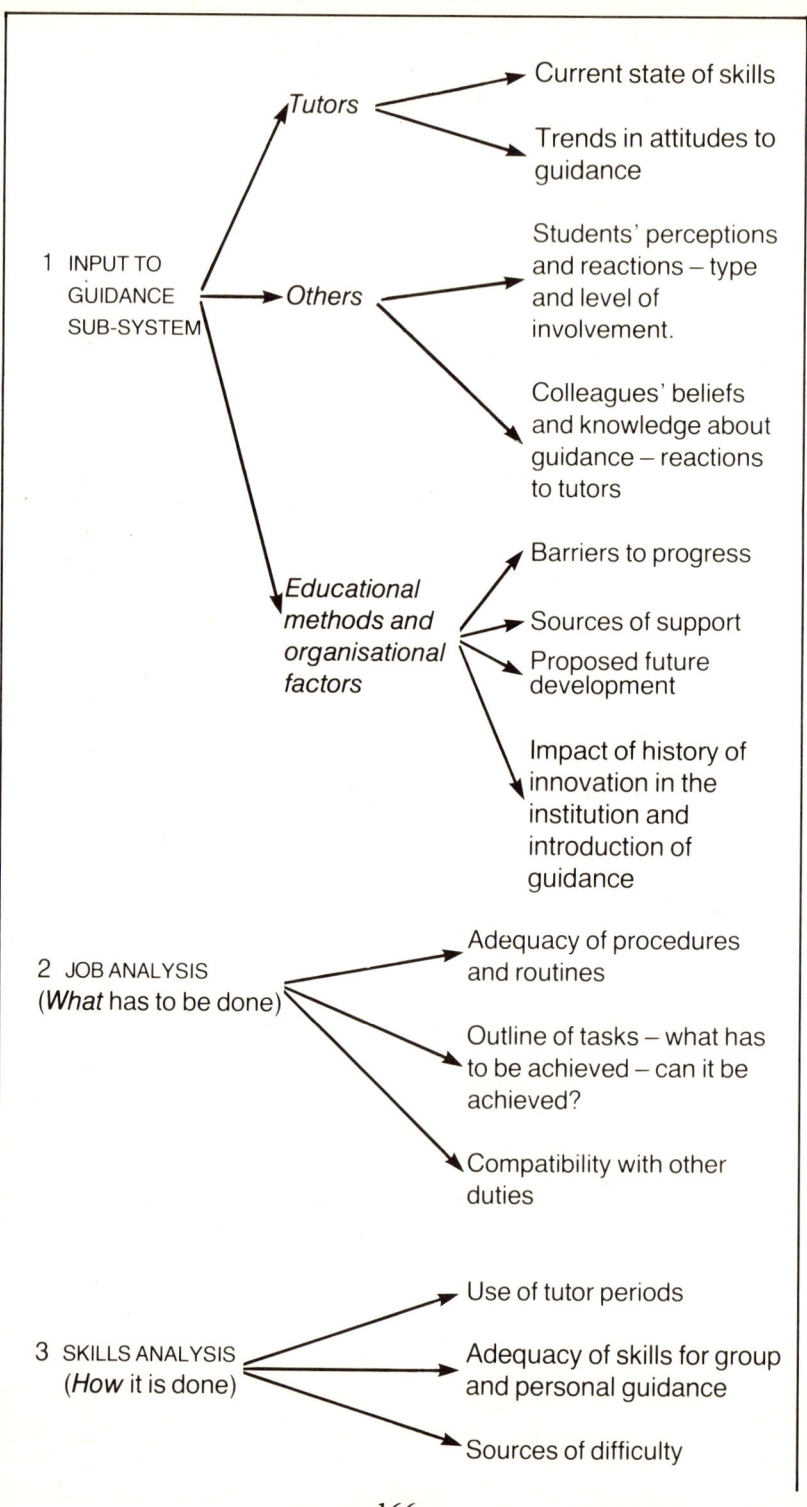

- *Tutors*
  - Current state of skills
  - Trends in attitudes to guidance
- *Others*
  - Students' perceptions and reactions – type and level of involvement.
  - Colleagues' beliefs and knowledge about guidance – reactions to tutors
- *Educational methods and organisational factors*
  - Barriers to progress
  - Sources of support
  - Proposed future development
  - Impact of history of innovation in the institution and introduction of guidance

2 JOB ANALYSIS (*What* has to be done)
- Adequacy of procedures and routines
- Outline of tasks – what has to be achieved – can it be achieved?
- Compatibility with other duties

3 SKILLS ANALYSIS (*How* it is done)
- Use of tutor periods
- Adequacy of skills for group and personal guidance
- Sources of difficulty

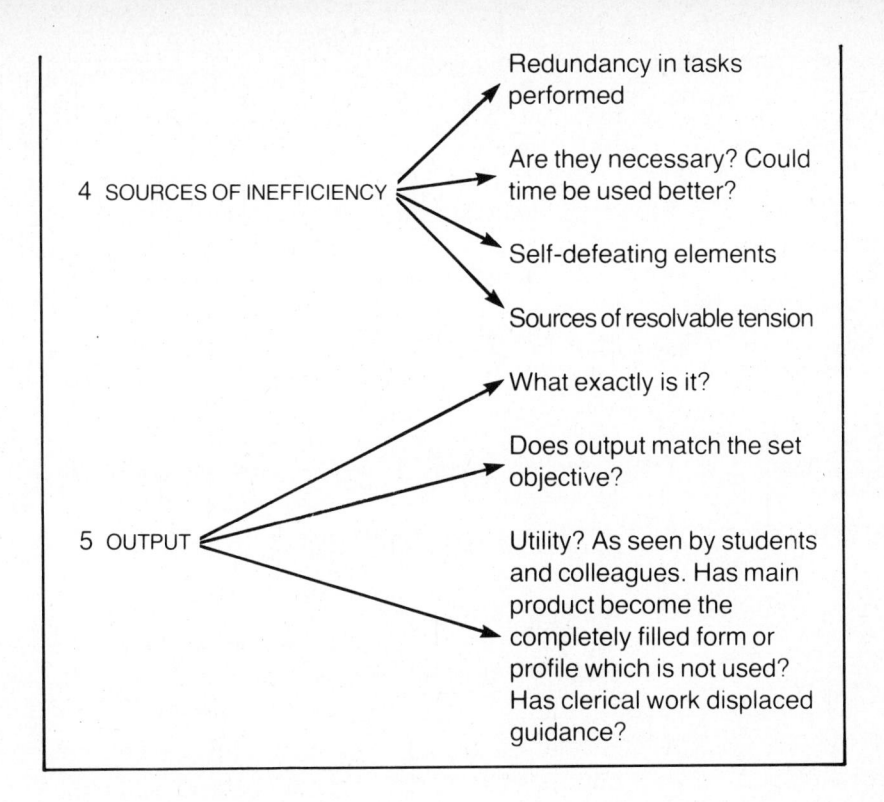

4 SOURCES OF INEFFICIENCY
- Redundancy in tasks performed
- Are they necessary? Could time be used better?
- Self-defeating elements
- Sources of resolvable tension

5 OUTPUT
- What exactly is it?
- Does output match the set objective?
- Utility? As seen by students and colleagues. Has main product become the completely filled form or profile which is not used? Has clerical work displaced guidance?

References

A B C in Action: (1981) London: Further Education Curriculum and Review Unit.

Ahlstrom, W. and Havighurst, R. (1971) *400 Losers*, San Francisco: Jossey-Bass.

Allen, T. and Whiteley, J. (1968) *Dimensions of Effective Counseling*, Columbus, Ohio: Merrill.

Argyis, C. and Schön, D. (1974) *Theory into Practice: Increasing Professional Effectiveness*, San Francisco: Jossey-Bass.

Asch, S. (1946) Forming Impressions of Personality, *Journal of Abnormal and Social Psychology*, *41*, pp. 258 - 290.

Bales, R. (1970) *Personality and Interpersonal Behavior*, New York: Holt, Rinehart and Winston.

Bateson, C., Jackson, D., Haley, J. and Weakland, J. (1956) Toward a Theory of Schizophrenia, *Behavioral Science*, *1*. pp. 251 - 264.

Bell, R. (1968) A Re-interpretation of the Direction of Effects in Studies of Socialization, *Psychology Review*, *75*, pp. 81 - 95.

Berlin, I. (1972) *Fathers and Children*, London: Oxford University Press.

Birnbaum, M. (1969) Sense and Nonsense About Sensitivity Training, *Saturday Review*, *52*, pp. 82 - 83.

Buss, A. (1980) *Self-Consciousness and Anxiety*, San Francisco: Freeman.

Campbell, M. (1981) Cited in: Kramer, J. (1982) An Exploratory Study of the Reactions of Young People to Unemployment in Wales. University College of Swansea. Unpublished M.Ed. Dissertation.

Caplovitz, D. (1979) *Making Ends Meet*, Beverley Hills: Sage.

Chapman, L. (1981) Integration of Handicapped Pupils Into the Comprehensive School. In: Hamblin, D. (Ed.) *Problems and Practice of Pastoral Care*, Oxford: Basil Blackwell.

Christie, R. and Geis, F. (1970) *Studies in Machiavellianism*, New York: Academic Press.

Clarke, L. (1980) *Transition from School to Work: A Critical Review of Research in United Kingdom*.

Davies, I. (1976) *Objectives in Curriculum Design*, London: McGraw-Hill.

Deutsch, M. (1973) *The Resolution of Conflict*, New Haven: Yale University Press.

Doherty, K. (1977) A Framework for the Evaluation of Pastoral Care, in Hamblin, D. (Ed.) *Problems and Practice of Pastoral Care*, Oxford: Blackwell.

Dosey, M. and Meisels, M. (1969) Personal Space and Self-Protection, *Journal of Personality and Social Psychology, II*, pp. 93 - 97.

Durkheim, E. (1933) *The Division of Labour In Society*, New York: Macmillan.

Dweck, C. and Licht, B. (1980) Learned Helplessness and Intellectual Achievement, in Garber, J. and Seligman, M. (Eds.) *Human Helplessness*, New York: Academic Press.

Edwards, J. and Morris, H. (1981) *The Employment Problems of Young People in Lewisham*, Köln: IFAPLAN (On behalf of the Commission of European Communities).

Evans, M. (1982) *A Study of the Perceptions of Pastoral Care Held by Teachers and Pupils*, University College of Swansea: unpublished M.Ed. dissertation.

Fantz, R. and Nevis, S. (1961) Pattern Preferences in Perceptual Cognitive Development in Early Infancy, *Merrill-Palmer Quarterly, 13*, pp. 77 - 108.

Fleming, D. and Lavercombe, S. (1982) Talking about Unemployment with School Leavers, *British Journal of Guidance and Counselling, 10*, No. 1, pp. 22 - 33.

Further Education Curriculum Review and Development Unit (1981) *Vocational Preparation*, London: Department of Education and Science.

Further Education Curriculum Review and Development Unit (1982) *Tutoring*, London: Department of Education and Science.

Garber, J. and Seligman, M. (1980) (Eds.) *Human Helplessness*, New York: Academic Press.

Goffman, E. (1959) *The Presentation of Self in Everyday Life*, New York: Doubleday Anchor.

Goffman, E. (1967) *Interaction Ritual*, London: Allen Lane.

Goffman, E. (1971) *Relations in Public*, London: Allen Lane.

Hamblin, D. (1974) *The Teacher and Counselling*, Oxford: Blackwell.

Hamblin, D. (1978) *The Teacher and Pastoral Care*, Oxford: Blackwell.

Hamblin, D. (1981) *Teaching Study Skills*, Oxford: Blackwell.

Hargreaves, D. (1982) *The Challenge for the Comprehensive School*, London: Routledge and Kegan Paul.

Hayes, J. (1971) *Occupational Perceptions and Occupational Information*, Bromsgrove: Institute of Careers Officers.

Heider, F. (1967) *The Psychology of Interpersonal Relations*, New York: Wiley.

Hildreth, A., Derogatis, L. and McCusker, K. (1971) Body Buffer Zone and Violence: A Reassessment and Confirmation, *American Journal of Psychiatry, 127*, pp. 1641 - 1645.

Hoggart, R. (1959) *The Uses of Literacy*, London: Chatto and Windus.

Hollander, E. (1964) *Leaders, Groups and Influence*, New York: Oxford University Press.

Hopson, B. and Hopson, C. (1973) *Exercises in Career Development*, Cambridge, CRAC.

Jahoda, M. (1958) *Current Concepts of Positive Mental Health: A Report*, (Joint Commission on Mental Illness and Health: Monograph Series No. 1.), New York: Basic Books.

John, D. (1980) *Leadership in Schools*, London: Heinemann.

Kelly, G. (1955) *The Psychology of Personal Constructs*, New York: Norton.

King, E., Moor, C. and Mundy, J. (1974) *Post Compulsory Education, Vol. I. A New Analysis of Western Europe, Vol. II. The Way Ahead*, London: Sage.

Klein, D. (1960) Some Concepts Concerning the Mental Health of the Individual, *Journal of Consulting Psychology*, 24, pp. 288 - 293.

Kogan, N. and Wallach, M. (1967) Risk Taking as a Function of the Situation, the Person and the Group, in *New Directions in Psychology, III*, New York: Holt, Rinehart and Winston.

Kramer, J. (1982) *An Exploratory Survey of the Reactions of Young People to Unemployment in Wales*, University College of Swansea: unpublished M.Ed. dissertation.

Krumboltz, J. and Thoresen, C. (1969) *Behavioral Counseling*, New York: Holt, Rinehart and Winston.

Laing, R., Phillipson, H. and Lee, A. (1966) *Interpersonal Perception*, London: Tavistock.

Lamm, H., Schaude, E. and Trommsdorf (1971) Risky Shift as a Function of Group Members' Value of Risk and Need for Approval, *Journal of Personality and Social Psychology*, 20, pp. 430 - 435.

Landfield, A. (1969) *Personal Construct Systems in Psychotherapy*, Chicago: Rand McNally.

Lickona, T. (1976) (Ed.) *Moral Development and Behaviour*, New York: Holt, Rinehart and Winston.

Lieberman, M., Yalom, I. and Miles, M. (1973) *Encounter Groups: First Facts*, New York: Basic Books.

Lowenfield, V. (1957) *Creative and Mental Growth*, New York: Macmillan. (3rd Edition.)

Lundberg, M. (1974) *The Incomplete Adult*, Westwood, Conn.: Greenwood Press.

Malinowski, B. (1922) *Argonauts of the Western Pacific*, London: Kegan Paul, Trench and Trubner.

Marland, M. (Ed.) (1981) *Information Skills in the Secondary School*, London: Methuen.

Mauss, M. (Translated: Cunnison, J. (1954) *The Gift: Forms and Functions of Exchange in Archaic Societies*, London; Cohen and West.

McCauley, C., Stitt, C., Woods, K. and Lipton, D. (1973) Group Shift to Caution at the Race Track, *Journal of Experimental Social Psychology*, 9, pp. 80 - 86.

Milgram, S. (1974) *Obedience to Authority*, London: Tavistock.

Moor, C. (1976) *From School to Work*, London: Sage.

Oppenheim, A. (1966) *Questionnaire Design and Attitude Measurement*, London: Heinemann.

Parker, J. and Rubin, L. (1966) *Process as Content: Curriculum Design and the Application of Knowledge*, Chicago: Rand McNally.

Parsons, T., Bales, R. and Shils, E. (1953) *Working Papers on the Theory of Action*, New York: Free Press.

Quicke, J. (1978) Rogerian Psychology and Non-Directive Counselling in Schools, *Educational Research*, Vol. 20, No. 3, pp. 192 - 200.

Read, H. (1958) *Education Through Art*, London: Faber and Faber.

Reddin, W. (1970) *Managerial Effectiveness*, New York: McGraw-Hill.

Rees, T. and Smith, G. (1980) *Co-ordinated Planning and the Transition from School to Work in Wales*, Working Paper No. 7, Cardiff: University College Sociological Research Unit.

Rogers, C. (1951) *Client-Centered Therapy*, Boston: Houghton Mifflin.

Rogers, C. (1961) *On Becoming a Person*, Boston: Houghton Mifflin.

Rommetweit, R. (1960) *Selectivity, Intuition and Halo Effects in Social Perception*, Oslo: Oslo University Press.

Rosenberg, M. (1979) *Conceiving the Self*, New York: Basic Books.

Rotter, J., Chance, J. and Phares, E. (1972) *Applications of a Social Learning Theory of Personality*, New York: Holt, Rinehart and Winston.

Rowe, D. (1978) *The Experience of Depression*, Chichester: Wiley.

Rubenowitz, S. (1968) *Emotional Flexibility – Rigidity as a Comprehensive Dimension of Mind*, Stockholm: Almquist and Wiksell.

Rutter, M. (1975) *Helping Troubled Children*, Harmondsworth: Penguin.

Sawdon, A., Pelican, J. and Tucker, S. (1981) *Study of the Transition from School to Working Life, Vols. II and III*, London: Youthaid.

Schaffer, H. and Emerson, P. (1964) *The Development of Social Attachments in Infancy*, Monographs of the Society for Research in Child Development, 29, 3. Serial No. 94.

School and After. A European Symposium, (1978) Windsor: NFER.

Schools Council Careers Education and Guidance Project (1978) *Work One, Work Two and Work Three*, London: Longman.

Smith, C. (1982) *A Study of Factors Influencing Sixth Form Students' Evaluation of Their Academic Work*, University College of Swansea: unpublished M.Ed. dissertation.

Snadowsky, A. (1973) *Child and Adolescent Development*, New York: Free Press.

Spivack, G., Platt, J. and Shure, M. (1976) *The Problem-Solving Approach to Adjustment*, San Francisco: Jossey Bass.

Taba, H. (1962) *Curriculum Development: Theory and Practice*, New York: Harcourt, Brace and World.

Taylor, D. (1981) *Innovation and Unemployment*, London: Youthaid.

Thompson Report (1982) *Experience and Participation:* Report of Review Group on the Youth Service in England, London: HMSO.

Thoresen, C. and Mahoney, M. (1974) *Behavioral Self-Control*, New York: Holt, Rinehart and Winston.

Turner, R. (1970) *Family Interaction*, New York: Wiley.

Ward, L. (Ed.) (1982) *The Ethical Dimension of the School Curriculum*, Swansea: Faculty of Education, University College of Swansea.

Watkins, C. (1981) Adolescents and Activities, in Hamblin, D. (Ed.) *Problems and Practice of Pastoral Care*, Oxford: Blackwell.

Watson, D. and Tharp, R. (1972) *Self-Directed Behaviour: Self-Modification for Personal Adjustment*, Monterey, Calif.: Brooks/Cole.

Welsh Office (1982) *Pastoral Care in the Comprehensive Schools of Wales*, Education Issues 3, Cardiff: HMSO.

Williams, J. (1971) *Personal Space and its Relation to Extroversion - Introversion*, Canadian Journal of Behavioural Science, 3. pp. 156 - 160.

Williams, K. (1973) *The School Counsellor*, London: Methuen.

Willis, P. (1978) *Learning to Labour*, Farnborough: Saxon House.

Zimbardo, P. (1969) *The Human Choice: Individuation, Reason and Order Versus Deinviduation, Impulse and Chaos* in Arnold, W. and Levine, D. (Eds.) *Nebraska Symposium on Motivation*, Lincoln: University of Nebraska Press.

Acknowledgements

The author and publishers wish to acknowledge the use of material from the following works:

Luchins, A. and Luchins, E. (1959) *Rigidity of Behaviour: A Variational Approach to the Effect of Einstellung*, Eugene: University of Oregon.

Peel, E. A. (1960) *The Pupil's Thinking*, London: Oldbourne. (p.101)

Index

Acceptance – signals of, 20
Aggression, 135-136
Ahlstrom, W., 17,18
Allen, T., 24
Anxiety:
   social, 104, 111-116
   audience, 111
Appraisal, 160
Argyis, C., 11
Asch, S., 126
Attribution, 2
Authority in pastoral care, 3

Bales, R., 49, 127
Bateson, C., 20
Bell, R., 9
Berlin, I., 4
Birnbaum, M., 6
Blame of others, 141
Buss, A., 111

Campbell, M., 81
Caplovitz, D., 92
Career guidance, 6-7
Careers education, 99-103
Causality, 12, 14
Chapman, L., 7
Christie, R., 9
Clarke, L., 68
Communication, 106-107, 109-110
Construct technique, 129-131
Co-operation, 124-126
Counselling:
   basic techniques, 17-21
   behavioural, 28-30
   reflecting back, 19
Creativity, 161-162

Davies, I., 10, 66, 163

Decision-making, 32-33, 55-56
Decision-making related
   to employment, 99-103
Depression, 93-94
Deutsch, M., 124
Diagrams in learning, 153-156
Distortions of
   pastoral care, 2-3
Doherty, K., 23, 163
Dosey, M., 131
Doublebind, 20-21
Durkheim, E., 7
Dweck, C., 159

Edwards, J., 86, 87
Embarrassment – social, 115-116
Emerson, P., 9
Employment, 6-8, 86-99
Entrepreneurial skills, 92-93
Entwistle, N., 36
Evaluation, 163
Evans, M., 3
Evidence – use of, 159
Exchange relationships, 7, 87, 91-93
Extinction, 29

Family relationships and
   unemployment, 93-97
Fantz, R., 9
Feelings – in counselling
   techniques, 18
Fixed role technique, 59-62
Fleming, D., 91
Frustration, 112, 117-118
Frustration in learning, 142

Games, 51-52
Garber, J., 12
Geis, F., 9

Goffman, E., 9
Group guidance:
  content, 64-66
  leadership of, 49-50
  limits to, 45
  structure, 46, 50, 62-64
  underfunctioning, 37, 10
Group interaction:
  communication, 105-107
  judgements, 126-127
  listening, 107-108
  opinion leaders, 133-134
  pairing, 133
  risks, 134-135
  three-dimensional model, 127-128

Hamblin, D., 36, 57, 129
Hargreaves, D., 3, 28
Havighurst, R., 17, 18
Hayes, J., 68
Heider, F., 12
Heim, A., 35
Helplessness – learned, 12-13, 159
Hidden curriculum, 5, 159
Hierarchy, 29
Hildreth, A., 131
Home influences, 42-43
Hoggart, R., 14
Hollander, E., 132
Hopson, B., 103
Hopson, C., 103

Identity – deviant, 2
Interview techniques, 21-24

Jahoda, M., 10, 11
Job:
  applications –
    forms, 82-83
    letters, 83
  generational confliction, 74
  interview skills, 80-81
  sanctions in working groups, 75-76
  search – mutual support during, 85
    – skills of, 78-81
John, D., 3

Kelly, G., 59, 128
King, E., 163
Klein, D., 11

Kogan, N., 134
Kramer, J., 87, 95, 97
Krumboltz, J., 28

Laing, R., 2
Lamm, H., 134
Landfield, A., 129
Lavercombe, S., 91
Leadership, 49, 131-132
Learning: 13-15
  attitudes to, 138-140
  beliefs about, 140
  self-defeating manoeuvres, 142
Leisure, 91
Lewis, D., 36
Licht, B., 159
Lickona, T., 111
Lieberman, M., 49
Life skills, 8
Life space diagram, 129
Listening skills, 107-108
Lowenfeld, V., 161
Luchins, A., 171

Mahoney, M., 28, 133
Malinowski, B., 7
Marland, M., 162
Mauss, M., 7
McCauley, C., 134
Meisels, M., 131
Mental Health, 10-11
Milgram, S., 124
Modules – of guidance, 15
Monitoring, 164-166
Moor, C., 68
Morris, H., 86, 87

Negotiation, 6, 10, 51
Nevis, S., 9
Normality – concept of, 11
Normative fallacy, 46
Norms, 45

Observation of group
  interaction, 133-134
Oppenheim, A., 160

Parker, J., 64
Parsons, T., 49
Peel, E., 171

Perception, 126
Personal space, 9, 131-132
Problem clarification, 31-32
Problem solving, 10
Problem solving in learning, 148-153

Questioning – constructive, 161
Questions:
  closed, 18
  double-barrelled, 23
  open, 18
Quicke, J., 45

Read, H., 161
Reading:
  checking approach to, 158-159
  structuring of, 156-158
Reddin, W., 46
Rees, T., 68
Reinforcement, 28
Responses– selection and
  evaluation, 24-28
Responsibility, 23, 28
Rigidity, 14
Rogers, C., 5, 11, 45, 46

Role play, 62
Roles, 45, 47, 48, 164
Rommetweit, R., 126
Rosenberg, M., 11
Rotter, J., 47, 104, 127
Rowe, D., 93
Rubenowvitz, S., 14
Rubin, L., 64
Rutter, M., 93

Sawden, A., 78
Schaffer, H., 9
Schon, D., 11
Self-management in
  learning, 141-142
Seligman, M., 12
Sexual stereotypes, 97
Simulations, 52-54
Smith, C., 141
Smith, G., 68
Snadowsky, A., 9
Social learning theory, 47, 104, 127
Social skills, 8-9, 116-126
Spivack, G., 10

Standpoint-taking, 10, 31-32, 123
Stimulus generalisation, 29
Stresses – occupational, 69
Success, 141

Taba, H., 64
Taylor, D., 7, 86
Telephone skills, 84
Tension management, 110
Tharp, R., 133
Thoresen, C., 28, 133
Thought:
  authoritarian, 143-144
  concrete, 14
  dogmatic, 144-145
  levelling and,
  sharpening, 145-147
  style of, 140
Touch, 9
Trigger situations, 29-31
Trust versus mistrust, 5-6
Trust walks, 9
Turner, R., 164

Under-functioning:
  case histories, 39-43
  strategy for exploring, 34-38
Unemployment:
  coach, 88
  effects, 86
  exchange relationships and, 87
  depression and, 93-94
  family relationships and, 93-97
  females, different impact on, 87
  leisure activities and, 91
  nature, 6-7

Wallach, M., 134
Watkins, C., 16
Ward, L., 111
Whiteley, J., 24
Williams, K., 163
Williams, J., 131
Willis, P., 68, 76
Work:
  adjustment to, 68-78
  dress at, 81
  stresses, 69

Zimbardo, P., 134